To Pave the Way for His People

A Life of Preston Taylor

Edward J. Robinson

A Project of the Disciples of Christ Historical Society

Copyright © 2024 by Edward J. Robinson

All rights reserved. For permission to reuse content, please contact the Disciples of Christ Historical Society.

Cover image: ©Disciples of Christ Historical Society
Cover and interior design: Connie H. C. Wang

Print: 9780827237360
EPUB: 9780827237377
EPDF: 9780827237384

Printed in the United States of America

Table of Contents

Acknowledgments	vii
A Chronology of Preston Taylor's Life	ix
Prologue. 'As Cool as a Brave Soldier'	xi
Part 1. From Slavery to Freedom, 1849–1869	1
1. 'We Are Here': The Formative Years	3
2. 'Freedom in My Bones': The Civil War	9
Part 2. Successes and Struggles in Kentucky, 1870–1884	19
3. 'His Highest Calling': Polity, Theology, and African American Disciples of Christ	21
4. Holding on to Jesus: African American Women in Disciples of Christ	43
Part 3. Trials and Triumphs in Tennessee, 1885–1916	59
5. 'Fighting the Devil in Nashville': The Complex World of African Americans in Middle Tennessee	61
6. A Resting Place and a Breathing Place: The Formation of Greenwood Cemetery and Greenwood Park	79
7. 'Riding the Goat': Civic Organizations in Black Nashville	95
8. Wrapped Up in the Lea Avenue Christian Church: Pastoral Ministry in Nashville	111

Part 4. Preston Taylor and the National Christian　　125
　　　Missionary Convention, 1917–1931

　　9. 'Onward Christian Soldiers':　　127
　　　　The National Christian Missionary Convention,
　　　　1917–1919

　　10. 'March on to Victory':　　141
　　　　The National Christian Missionary Convention,
　　　　1920–1931

Epilogue. 'He Led the Way'　　157

Bibliography　　161

Index　　169

To:

Rick Lowery,

brother, colleague, and friend

And to the memory of:

John L. Robinson

(1935-2022)

Acknowledgments

This book would have been impossible without the following people: Teresa "Terri" Hord Owens, General Minister and President of the Christian Church (Disciples of Christ), Rick Lowery, past President of the Disciples of Christ Historical Society (DCHS), Joel Brown, current President of DCHS, Thaddaeus Allen, Rebecca Hale, Jamey Gorman, Valerie Melvin, Janae Pitts-Murdock, K. J. Kim, Lisa Barnett, Shelley L. Jacobs, and Jim McMillan—all of these good people are connected in some way to the DCHS in Bethany, West Virginia; and all of them affirmed me in my efforts to write this book.

In 2004, my brief entry on Preston Taylor was published in the *Encyclopedia of the Stone-Campbell Movement*. Over the years, I copied and filed away materials on this dynamic leader, but the documents lay dormant. The Preston Taylor materials might have remained stashed away in my bags and files had it not been for Rick Lowery, who urged me to pursue this biography.

Of course, my books, *Show Us How You Do It: Marshall Keeble and the Rise of Black Churches of Christ, 1914-1968* (University of Alabama Press, 2008) and *Hard-Fighting Soldiers: A History of African American Churches of Christ* (University of Tennessee Press, 2019), reference Preston Taylor, the preacher for the Lea Avenue Christian Church (Disciples of Christ), for baptizing Marshall Keeble, who eventually emerged as the premier evangelist in African American Churches of Christ.

In 2022, Dr. Rick Lowery graciously invited me to join the Board of Trustees of the Disciples of Christ Historical Society; in the same year, I gave a lecture on Preston Taylor at the Kirkpatrick Conference in Tulsa, Oklahoma, which was hosted by the Historical Society. During this conference, several participants, including Dr. Lawrence Burnley, Dr. Charisse L. Gillett, Rev. Gary Kidwell, among many others, encouraged me to pursue a book-length treatment of Taylor.

Many thanks to Mac Ice, Shelley Jacobs, and librarians at Abilene Christian University, University of Texas at Tyler, Texas College, and the Tyler Public Library—who assisted me in obtaining books and sources via Inter-Library Loan. Doug Foster and Jamey Gorman read versions of the manuscript and gave me valuable critical insight to improve the book.

My wife, Toni, has once again supported me in this endeavor; and my daughter, Ashley, did significant detective work and helped me track down important bits and pieces of crucial information. Her efforts enabled me to put together missing pieces of this biographical puzzle. Thank you, Ashley!

My good friend and mentor, Dr. John L. Robinson, fell ill and could not read the manuscript. John sadly passed away on August 10, 2022. "John, I think you would be proud of this!" I gratefully dedicate this book to the memory of John L. Robinson and to the honor of Rick Lowery.

A Chronology of Preston Taylor (1849–1931)

1849	Born in Shreveport, Louisiana
1850	Family moved to Kentucky
1864	Became a drummer boy in the 116th United States Colored Troops (USCT)
1867	Ushered out of the 116th USCT
1869	Confessed faith in Christ
1870	Settled in Kentucky and worked as porter on the railroad
	Married Ella Spradling and later divorced
1871	Began preaching for the Christian Church in Mt. Sterling, Kentucky
1873	Organized a Christian Church at Millersburg, Kentucky
1879	Began writing for the *Christian Leader*
1880	Married and later divorced Anna Hoffman
1885	Relocated from Kentucky to Nashville, Tennessee
1886	Became pastor of the Gay Street Christian Christ in Nashville
1887	Featured in *Men of Mark*, by William J. Simmons
1888	Opened a funeral home in Nashville; later called Taylor Funeral Home
1890–1891	Withdrew from Gay Street Christian Church and formed Lea Avenue Christian Church

1890	Married Georgia Gordon in Nashville, Tennessee
1903	Completed the edifice for Lea Avenue Christian Church
1904	Opened One Cent Savings Bank & Trust Company
1905	Established Greenwood Park in Nashville
1906	Featured in *The Negro in Business* by Booker T. Washington
1909	Helped establish Tennessee State University
1913	Third wife, Georgia Gordon Taylor, died
1916	Married his fourth wife, Ida Mallory
1917	Organized the National Christian Missionary Convention in Nashville
1919	Featured in *The National Cyclopedia of the Colored Race*
1931	Died in Nashville, Tennessee
1947	Fourth wife, Ida Mallory Taylor, died
1951	Housing project dedicated to Preston Taylor's memory in Nashville, Tennessee

Prologue

'As Cool as a Brave Soldier'

Two days into the New Year of 1892, a 5:40 evening fire alarm summoned firemen to the seven-story Phillips-Buttorff Building in downtown Nashville, Tennessee. Upon arriving at the engulfed structure, Fire Chief Caroll hastily organized his crew to combat the flames. The hook and ladder team took their place after an African American driver, Jesse Brooks, climbed on the ladder. Two hours after the initial fire bell sounded, two white and four black fire fighters made their way to the roof of the Phillips-Buttorff Building; but curious and concerned spectators below saw walls of the adjacent Warren Building swaying and sent up a "great shout of warning" to the firemen. George Thomas and his white comrade heard and heeded the onlookers' warning. When Thomas turned back to alert his four African American cohorts, the "Warren building crashed over on the Phillips-Buttorff structure, sweeping three of the firemen down to instant death."[1]

George Thomas suffered injuries, but he survived. Aaron Cockrill, another black fireman, saw the collapsing wall "in time to get out of its reach." The three victims—thirty-nine-year-old Captain Charles C. Gowdy, forty-one-year-old Hardy Ewing, and twenty-nine-year-old Stokely H. Allen—died heroically. *The Daily American* reported: "The members of the gallant colored fire company worked disconsolately but manfully at the fire after the horrible death of their comrades. And the white firemen also felt the loss of the brave men who had

---

[1] "Fire and Death," *Daily American* (January 3, 1892): 1. Eugene Lewis launched the *Daily American* or *Nashville American* in 1876, and it continued operation until 1911, when it was acquired by *The Tennessean.* See John Egerton, *Nashville: The Faces of Two Centuries, 1780–1980* (Nashville, TN: PlusMedia, 1979), 170. William Waller, ed., *Nashville in the 1890s* (Nashville, TN: Vanderbilt University Press, 1970), 277. Waller noted that, altogether, eleven firemen were injured and property damaged was approximately $600,000.

so bravely and so often fought the flames with them side by side."[2] In a segregated Southern city, the tragic demise of the three African American fire fighters helped to unite a racially divided community, even if temporarily.

Rescuers recovered the bodies of Allen and Ewing from the debris the following day. Investigators identified their remains by the keys in their pocket vests. A key taken from Ewing's vest opened his locker at the fire station. *The Daily American* then noted that, "Allen was further identified by the ring found on the hand picked up near his charred trunk."[3]

But sympathetic residents of Nashville wondered if investigators would ever find the remains of Captain Gowdy. After digging and searching all day Sunday, the local newspaper commented that the workers became "discouraged, and a few, convinced that Gowdy had been entirely cremated, ceased operations before daybreak yesterday morning." Yet on Monday afternoon, an inspector stumbled upon Gowdy's corpse, and the coroner noted that it was in much better condition than Allen's and Ewing's, "but nonetheless sickening to behold." "The remains of one of the hands," the paper observed, "were clasped about the brass nozzle that he held when last seen in life." After Gowdy's body was recovered and placed in a "small pine box," the "scene of interest was transferred to Taylor's undertaking establishment,"[4] owned and operated by Preston Taylor.

When asked to share his thoughts about the deaths of the three martyrs, Fire Chief Caroll lamented, "It is just so with the fireman's life. When the bell strikes and we leave the house, we know not whether we will ever return. It is, indeed, a hazardous business." Mayor George Guild, aware of the heroic sacrifices made by the firefighters, proclaimed Tuesday (January 5) a "day of mourning," as he bestowed "civic honors" on the three deceased black firemen. The following day, thousands of mourners and admirers braved inclement weather, lined the streets, and witnessed the large and extravagant funeral procession, as it meandered to Mount Ararat Cemetery, where the "dead heroes slept beautifully in their cold and silent graves."[5]

---

[2] "Fire and Death," 1.
[3] "Desolate Ruins," *Daily American* (January 4, 1892): 1.
[4] "Heroic Until the End," *Daily American* (January 7, 1892): 5.
[5] "Laid to Rest," *Daily American* (January 7, 1892): 5.

All three victims—Gowdy, Ewing, and Allen—were young married men with children, active in the community, and deeply religious. The three corpses were charred and disfigured, but for Preston Taylor, the lives and bodies of black people mattered. Indeed, the *Daily American* reported, "Undertaker Preston Taylor had entire charge of all the funeral arrangements yesterday and the perfections with which they were carried out elicited much favorable comment." Silver handles on the coffins, the paper added, were the "finest that could be held in the city," and the funeral proceedings were "admirably carried out to the minutest detail."[6]

These brief statements succinctly capture the essence of Preston Taylor's life, and they furnish the thesis for this book. Taylor was a consummate professional, committed to excellence in the service of all people—especially black people. More than two decades after the 1892 conflagration, Nashville residents still remembered his leadership and professionalism. A leading black newspaper commented in 1913:

> There are few homes in the wide city of Nashville that when the angel of death hovered over them, have [sic] in 1892, when the gallant Gowdy, Ewing, and Allen sacrificed their lives to save this city. On the occasion of that funeral, the whole city was bowed down in mourning and seemed impossible for any one to have enough physical strength to handle so mammoth a crowd as assembled at the State Capitol on the day of the funeral.

Inundated with grief and sorrow, the *Nashville Globe* recalled that Taylor was "as cool as a brave soldier on the battlefield, and the way he handled that funeral won for him the admiration of the entire citizenship of Nashville."[7] Taylor led a grief-stricken community through a community-wide misfortune, and yet the horrible and dark tragedy paradoxically lifted Taylor to local and regional fame; his work as a church and community leader would eventually catapult him to national prominence.

Although a handful of works have made brief references to Taylor regarding his formation of Greenwood Park and Greenwood

---

[6] Ibid.

[7] "Quarter of a Century's Progress," *Nashville Globe* (April 11, 1913): 5. The *Nashville Globe*, formed in 1905, promoted black pride and self-sufficiency. See Egerton, *Nashville*, 192.

Cemetery and the transportation protest in Nashville in 1905,[8] this book offers the first full-length academic study of this religious trailblazer and social reformer who, while working to expand the geographic reach of African American Disciples of Christ, found time to assist in the racial uplift of fellow black people. This book argues that the military experience he acquired as a drummer boy in the Civil War furnished the foundation for all of his future endeavors as a church leader and community activist. Throughout his adult life, he remained a brave and loyal soldier, one who championed the causes of economic advancement, social justice, educational development for young people, and recreational facilities for African Americans in Middle Tennessee and beyond.

One contemporary and influential publication called Taylor a "man of nerve and iron-will determined to pave the way for his people." On the one hand, he was a devout member of the Stone-Campbell movement,[9] a religious campaign from the early

---

[8] Charlotte A. Williams, *The Centennial Club of Nashville: A History from 1905-77* (Nashville, TN: Centennial Club, 1978), 50. Egerton, *Nashville*, 191–192. Don H. Doyle, *Nashville in the South, 1880-1930* (Knoxville, TN: University of Tennessee Press, 1985), 110, 118–119. Leland R. Johnson, *The Parks of Nashville: A History of the Board of Parks and Recreation* (Nashville, TN: Board of Parks and Recreation, 1986), 45, 242. Terry Weeks and Bob Womack, *Tennessee: The History of an American State* (Montgomery, AL: Clairmont Press, 1996), 291. Bobby L. Lovett, *The African-American History of Nashville, Tennessee, 1780–1930* (Fayetteville, AR: University of Arkansas Press, 1999), 115, 117, 184–185.

[9] Clement Richardson, *The National Cyclopedia of the Colored Race* (Montgomery, AL: National Publishing Company, 1919), 334. The Stone-Campbell movement, a phrase coined by Leroy Garrett in 1981, traces its origins to the early nineteenth century and to four principal leaders: Barton W. Stone (1772–1844), Thomas Campbell (1763–1854), Alexander Campbell (1788–1866), and Walter Scott (1796–1861). These men championed the unity of all believers in Christ based on the Bible alone. Useful reference works include Douglas A. Foster, *A Life of Alexander Campbell* (Grand Rapids, MI: Eerdmans, 2020). James L. Gorman, *Among the Early Evangelicals: The Transatlantic Origins of the Stone-Campbell Movement* (Abilene, TX: Abilene Christian University Press, 2017). Douglas A. Foster, Paul M. Blowers, Anthony L. Dunnavant, and D. Newell Williams (eds.), *The Encyclopedia of the Stone-Campbell Movement* (Grand Rapids, IN: Eerdmans, 2004). David Harrell Harrell, Jr., *Sources of Division in the Disciples of Christ, 1865–1900* (Tuscaloosa, AL: University of Alabama Press, 1973/2003). Richard T. Hughes, *Reviving the Ancient Faith: The Story of Churches of Christ in America* (Grand Rapids, MI: Eerdmans, 1996). Leroy Garrett, *The Stone-Campbell Movement: An Anecdotal History of Three Churches* (Joplin, MO: College Press, 1981/1987).

nineteenth century seeking to "restore" New Testament Christianity. On the other hand, his ecumenical views led him to join hands with black Baptists, Methodists, and other religionists to uplift African Americans and to contest racial proscriptions in Middle Tennessee and beyond.

I have organized this book chronologically and topically into four parts with ten chapters. The first chapter probes Taylor's sojourn from chattel enslavement in Louisiana to emancipation in Kentucky. The second assesses his involvement in the Civil War as a drummer boy and the war's lingering influence on his career as a minister and community worker. Chapter 3 appraises his ecclesiological and theological perspectives as a pastor in Mt. Sterling, Kentucky, and the next chapter examines how African American women inspired Taylor, as well as the role these women played in the growth and development of African American Disciples of Christ. Chapter 5 describes the racial climate in which Taylor and black Nashvillians toiled. Chapter 6 explores Taylor's efforts to build a burial place and a recreational facility for black people in Nashville. Chapters 7 and 8 survey his work as a community activist and a local pastor with the Lea Avenue Christian Church. The last two chapters assess Taylor's leadership role in the National Christian Missionary Convention (NCMC) from 1917 until his death in 1931.

In this book, I use the phrases, *Christian Church* and *Disciples of Christ*, interchangeably to refer to the group tracing their origins back to the work of Barton W. Stone and Alexander Campbell. Taylor sometimes used the designation *Church of Christ* to identify his chosen fellowship, the Christian Church (Disciples of Christ). Churches of Christ—opposing the use of instruments in worship, lofty religious titles, and missionary societies—severed ties from the Disciples of Christ in the early twentieth century. Taylor aligned himself with the latter group, the group that endorsed using musical instruments in worship, open fellowship, missionary societies, and other extra-congregational activities.[10]

Over his eight-decade lifespan, Preston Taylor yielded extraordinary exploits, yet he was not superhuman. His unique mix of fairness and firmness, grit and grace, and compassion and passion perhaps led to both his triumphs and his troubles. Four marriages

---

[10] Robert E. Hooper, *A Distinct People: A History of the Churches of Christ in the 20th Century* (West Monroe, LA: Howard Publishing, 1993).

intimate that an immature Taylor—endowed with charm, charisma, and good looks—was not ready to settle down during his younger days. Notwithstanding his flaws and imperfections, an assessment of his exceptional life opens a clear window into his world as well as to our own twenty-first-century world.

As a black man in the United States, Taylor imbibed what scholar W. E. B. Du Bois has called "double-consciousness." Du Bois explained, "One ever feels his twoness,—an American, a Negro; two souls, two thoughts, two unreconciled strivings; two warring ideals in one dark body, whose dogged strength alone keeps it from being torn asunder."[11] Taylor also fluctuated between the "dialectical polarities" of "other-worldly versus this-worldly," propounded by historians C. Eric Lincoln and Lawrence H. Mamiya.[12] On one hand, Taylor urged fellow African American believers to "lay up their treasures in heaven." On the other hand, he strongly agitated for the civil rights of black people and worked diligently to address their social and material needs. This spiritual and social oscillation makes for a complex man in complicated times.

Taylor toiled first and foremost as a Christian clergyman, but he was so much more: a funeral director, proprietor, mason, military veteran, stockholder in a local bank, philanthropist, and advocate of social justice. He was arguably one of the most prominent African American leaders in the Progressive Era, and he was unquestionably the most visible and influential black man in the Stone-Campbell movement from Reconstruction to the Great Depression. Yet regrettably, his story has been buried beneath the sand dunes of history. This work seeks, therefore, to rescue Preston Taylor from historical obscurity and place him on the pedestal of acclaim, with all his successes, faults, and failures.

---

[11] W. E. B. Du Bois, *The Souls of Black Folk* (New York: Signet Classics, 1903/2012), 9.

[12] C. Eric Lincoln and Lawrence H. Mamiya, *The Black Church in the African American Experience* (Durham, NC: Duke University Press, 1990), 12. Lincoln and Mamiya argued: "'Other-worldly' means being concerned only with heaven and eternal life or the world beyond, a pie-in-the-sky attitude that neglects political and social concerns. 'This-worldly' refers to involvement in the affairs of the world, especially politics and social life, in the here and now." See also, Anne H. Pinn and Anthony B. Pinn, *Fortress Introduction to Black Church History* (Minneapolis: Fortress Press, 2002), 15–16.

Part 1

From Slavery to Freedom, 1849-1869

One

'We Are Here'

The Formative Years of Preston Taylor

Stand fast therefore in the liberty wherewith Christ hath made us free, and be not entangled again with the yoke of bondage.

—Galatians 5:1

In the fall of 1849, Frederick Douglass, a prominent African American abolitionist, published an article in his antislavery newspaper, *The North Star*, and fussed that the black man was not "permitted to carry a United States' mail bag across the street, nor hand it from a stage-driver to a post-master." Racial hatred, he added, precluded a black man from the military: "[N]o matter how daring, heroic, and patriotic he may be, he is forbidden, by the government, to rise above the office of a cook, or a steward, under the flag of the United States."[1] These assertions reveal that enslaved people often faced severe restrictions, with limited mobility and limited opportunities in antebellum America.

Two days before Douglass issued his lament, Preston Taylor entered the world of chattel enslavement in antebellum Louisiana. Born on November 7, 1849, he emerged into a turbulent and chaotic world, reeling on the heels of the publication of Frederick Douglass's narrative, the annexation of Texas, and the Wilmot Proviso, which Pennsylvania Congressman David Wilmot proposed to ban chattel

---

[1] Frederick Douglass, "Government and Its Subjects," *The North Star* (November 9, 1849), cited in Philip S. Foner, *Frederick Douglass: Selected Speeches and Writings* (Chicago: Lawrence Hill, 1999), 147.

enslavement in the territory acquired from Mexico in the Mexican-American War. All of these tumultuous events helped fan the flames of the issue of slavery in a greater way. Indeed, the Mexican-American War, America's first foreign conflict, generated waves of excitement among black bondspeople in Louisiana. Solomon Northup, an enslaved black man in Louisiana for twelve years, recalled, "During the Mexican war I well remember the extravagant hopes that were excited," adding that most fellow enslaved people would welcome "with unmeasured delight the approach of an invading army."[2]

Notwithstanding Northup's observation, Preston Taylor's life as an enslaved person remains shrouded in mystery. Circumstantial evidence suggests he was born on a plantation owned by U.S. President Zachary Taylor. Known as "Old Rough and Ready," Zachary Taylor established impressive military records in the War of 1812 and the Black Hawk War, before emerging as a principal hero in the Mexican-American War of 1846–1848. Like George Washington, Andrew Jackson, William H. Harrison, and others before him, Zachary Taylor's military exploits helped pave the way to the White House.[3]

In 1838, the war hero paid cash for 163 acres of land in West Feliciana Parish, Louisiana; he then imported twenty-one enslaved black people from his Kentucky farms to Louisiana.[4] He owned the plantation until the 1840s, and he claimed to have possessed 300 enslaved people at one time.[5] Some sources indicate that his slaves were well fed, well clothed, and well cared for.[6] However, the testimony of Solomon Northup, an enslaved man in Louisiana, gives

---

[2] Solomon Northup, *Twelve Years a Slave* (New York: Dover, 1854/1970), 249.

[3] Silas Bent McKinley and Silas Bent, *Old Rough and Ready: The Life and Times of Zachary Taylor* (New York: Vanguard, 1946), 105–120, 135–148, 201–219.

[4] Holman Hamilton, *Zachary Taylor: Soldier of the Republic* (Indianapolis: Bobbs-Merrill, 1941), 72.

[5] McKinley and Bent, *Old Rough and Ready*, 208. They provided the following story: "A Louisiana planter wrote, 'I have worked hard and been frugal all my life, and the results of my industry have mainly taken the form of slaves, of whom I own about a hundred. Before I vote for President, I want to be sure that the candidate I support will not act so as to divest me of my property.' General Taylor replied: 'I have the honor to inform you that I too have been all my life industrious and frugal, and that the fruits thereof are mainly invested in slaves, of whom I own three hundred.'"

[6] See "General Taylor's Residence at Baton Rouge," *Harper's New Monthly Magazine* IX (1845): 764.

us reason to question such reports. Northup recalled drinking from the "bitter cup of slavery." He wailed, "Oh! How heavily the weight of slavery pressed upon me then." Like Job, Jeremiah, and other biblical patriarchs, Northup questioned God: "Why had I not died in my young years—before God had given me children to love and live for?" He further testified that he often worked with one eye on his work and the other one on his master. Enslaved black women were consistently subjected to "lust and hate"—lust from the white sexual predators and hatred from the wives of slaveholders. Such firsthand experiences prompted Northup to conclude: "There may be humane masters, as there certainly are inhuman ones—there may be slaves well-clothed, well-fed, and happy, as there are those half-clad, half-starved and miserable; nevertheless, the institution that tolerates such wrongs and inhumanity as I have witnessed, is a cruel, unjust, and barbarous one."

Additionally, a medical doctor in the Bayou State noted that the diet of the state's enslaved people consisted of cornbread, molasses, and salt pork, with very little "fresh meat and vegetables." Another white Louisianian observed that most slaves fell ill because they were overworked and slept in "crowded dirty apartments."[7]

Notwithstanding the conflicting testimony, we know for certain that Zachary Taylor in March of 1849 ascended to the presidency, and then he died seventeen months later. His estate—totaling $116,770.02 in cash, property, and slaves—was divided between his wife Margaret Taylor and their children. Twenty-three slaves became the property of Ann (Taylor) Wood; twenty-five fell into the hands of Betty (Taylor) Bliss; and eighty-three came into the possession of Richard Taylor.[8]

Preston Taylor was likely sired by a white man and an enslaved woman connected to the Taylor family, making him one of the 406,000 "new people" in the Antebellum South. We do not know the exact identity of his parents, Zed and Betty Taylor, who were of evidently light complexion, suggesting that Preston likely benefited

---

[7] Northup, *Twelve Years a Slave*, 121, 125, 131, 189, 206. The quote from the medical doctor appears in Kenneth M. Stampp, *The Peculiar Institution: Slavery in the Antebellum South* (New York: Vintage Books, 1956), 208, 285, 294 (quote).

[8] Jack Bauer, *Zachary Taylor: Soldier, Planter, Statesman of the Old Southwest* (Baton Rouge, LA: Louisiana State University Press, 1985), 320.

from the "mulatto advantage,"[9] which allowed him and other lighter-skinned enslaved people to eat better food, wear better clothing, and receive better health care and greater literacy opportunities. These biracial children became leaders and "great carriers of whiteness" into the African American community. Furthermore, sources on race relations attest that bisexual mixing was rife in pre–Civil War Louisiana.[10]

In 1882, Preston Taylor, when writing for the *Christian Standard*, announced the passing of his sixty-seven-year-old mother, who died of dropsy.[11] Regrettably, he furnished no detailed information about her parents or even his father's background. The *Nashville Banner* gave a summary of Taylor's life after he passed away on April 13, 1931; the paper reported that he was "owned by the family of Zed Taylor, a brother of former President Zachariah Taylor."[12] The paper misspelled the twelfth president's first name and erroneously said that Preston Taylor was a drummer boy in the Confederate Army, when he clearly sided with the Union cause.

In spite of the paucity of information on Taylor's childhood and adolescent years, his relation to the lineage of Zachary Taylor is undeniable; and as the president's estate was split up, his owners relocated the infant Preston, his parents, and other slaves from Louisiana to Kentucky in the 1850s. There is no extant evidence to show how Taylor and his family were treated as bondspeople. The family of future Supreme Court Justice John Marshall Harlan owned enslaved people in Danville, Kentucky, and reportedly treated them gingerly and cordially. On the other hand, the evidence is clear that the mid-nineteenth century proved volatile, with the so-called "decade of polarization." The Compromise of 1850, the publication of *Uncle Tom's Cabin*, the Kansas–Nebraska Act, the Brooks–Sumner Affair, the Dred Scott Case, the Lincoln–Douglas debates, and John Brown's Raid all triggered shockwaves throughout the country and

---

[9] Joel Williamson, *New People: Miscegenation and Mulattoes in the United States* (New York: The Free Press, 1980), 24. Howard Bodenhorn, "The Mulatto Advantage: The Biological Consequences in Rural Antebellum Virginia," *Journal of Interdisciplinary History* 33 (Summer 2002): 21–46.

[10] Williamson, *New People*, 130. The story of Patrick and Mulkey is cited in Stampp, *The Peculiar Institution*, 354.

[11] Preston Taylor, "Our Colored Brethren" *Christian Standard* 17 (January 21, 1882): 19.

[12] "Preston Taylor's Rites Thursday" *Nashville Banner* (April 16, 1931): 16.

eventually divided the nation over the enslavement of black people. One scholar has recently noted, "Chief among the forces driving and shaping those changes [in the 1850s] was the struggle over slavery's future."[13]

In addition, the connection of Preston Taylor to President Zachary Taylor is both significant and symbolic in that the former was born in the Bayou State, but he grew up in the Bluegrass State, just as the latter was born in Virginia but was reared in Kentucky. Indeed, authors Silas Bent McKinley and Silas Bent noted that when President Taylor passed away,

> The funeral carriage was drawn by eight white horses, each led by a Negro garbed in white. The massive wheels of the bier were black entwined with spangled white satin. ... Many detachments of troops and civic organizations were a part of the long parade, and the three-mile route to the Congressional cemetery was thickly lined with spectators.[14]

These words profoundly and paradoxically presaged the future life's work of Preston Taylor. Preston Taylor would later rise as an influential funeral director and lead numerous funeral processions with decked out carriages and beautiful horses to comfort and dignify bereaved black families and grief-stricken communities. It is almost as if Taylor was destined to emerge from a renowned presidential family and bestow honor and prestige on his own people—African Americans.

After his family relocated to Kentucky, Taylor reportedly heard his first sermon at age four and immediately expressed his desire to be a preacher. He was a precocious child, yet mischievous in that

---

[13] Bruce Levine, *Thaddeus Stevens: Civil War Revolutionary, Fighter for Racial Justice* (New York: Simon & Schuster, 2021), 94. Williamson, *New People*, 57, pointed out, "As masters moved west, they took their slaves with them, mulatto as well as black." For reference to how the Harlan family treated enslaved people, see Peter S. Canellos, *The Great Dissenter: The Story of John Marshall Harlan, America's Judicial Hero* (New York: Simon & Schuster, 2021), 94–95.

[14] Cited in McKinley and Bent, *Old Rough and Ready*, 288. Scholar Jonathan W. White, *A House Built by Slaves: African Americans Visitors to the Lincoln White House* (New York: Rowman & Littlefield, 2022), xx. White observed, "Slaves did, indeed, play a central role in the construction of the Executive Mansion. And from Thomas Jefferson to Zachary Taylor, Southern presidents brought enslaved people with them to work in the White House."

his mother once rebuked him for stealing a sweet treat, and she admonished him against theft. The young man humbly accepted his mother's verbal scolding, and as a teenager, he confessed faith in Christ and received baptism.[15] This account offers insight into what probably sustained young Taylor during the decade leading up to the Civil War. His mother's protective care and moral guidance—coupled with his burgeoning faith, keen intellect, and desire for church leadership—succored him during his tumultuous adolescent days.

Frederick Douglass captured the unshakeable resolve of Taylor and countless other enslaved persons who transitioned from slavery to freedom, when he asserted:

> *We are here,* and here we are likely to be. To imagine that we shall ever be eradicated is absurd and ridiculous. We can be remodified, changed, and assimilated, but never extinguished. We repeat, therefore, that we are here; and that this is our country; and the question for the philosophers and statesmen of the land ought to be, "What principles should dictate the policy of the action towards us?[16]

Douglass composed the foregoing article nine days after Preston Taylor's birth, and the former unwittingly presaged the essence of the latter's life. Like Douglass, Taylor would emerge as an influential civic leader and a powerful churchman in Middle Tennessee and beyond, determined never to be "extinguished" or "eradicated." He grew up in a chaotic world convinced he could accomplish anything and that this was his country, too. More than a mere talker, Taylor was a man of action, and he demonstrated his commitment to his people and to his nation by signing up to fight in the Civil War.

---

[15] Clement Richardson (ed.), *The National Cyclopedia of the Colored Race* (Montgomery, AL: National Publishing, 1919), 334. Todd W. Simmons, "Preston Taylor: Seeker of Dignity for Black Disciples," *Discipliana* 60 (Winter 2000): 100.

[16] Frederick Douglass, "The Destiny of Colored Americans" *The North Star* (November 16, 1849); cited in Foner, *Frederick Douglass*, 149.

Two

'Freedom in My Bones'

The Civil War

> Thou therefore endure hardness, as a good soldier of Jesus Christ. —2 Timothy 2:3
>
> Then came before me my relation to the slave. I had shared in the fruits of his unrequited toil; he was blind and dumb, and there was no one to plead for him.
>
> "Love thy neighbor as thyself" rang in my ears.
> —John G. Fee

Five days before Christmas in 1860, South Carolina became the first Southern state to secede from the Union. Eighteen days later, Mississippi withdrew from the federal government, arguing, "Our position is thoroughly identified with the institution of slavery—the greatest material interest in the world. Its labor supplies the product which constitutes by far the largest and most important portions of commerce of the earth." Mississippi legislators added that a "blow to slavery is a blow at commerce and civilization." Florida, Alabama, Georgia, Louisiana, and Texas soon followed the lead of South Carolina and Mississippi.[1]

Texas lawmakers, feeling betrayed by the federal government, became the seventh state to break away from the Union. On February 2, 1861, they vehemently expressed their desire to abandon the

---

[1] David M. Potter, *The Impending Crisis, 1848–1861* (New York: Harper & Row, 1976), 498.

Union because "the servitude of the African to the white race within her limits—a relation that had existed from the first settlement of her wilderness by the white race, and which her people intended should exist in all future time." These seven states comprised the Confederate States of America before adding Virginia, Arkansas, Tennessee, and North Carolina.[2]

On April 12, 1861, Confederate troops fired on Fort Sumter in South Carolina, igniting the bloodiest war in our nation's history. Some 532 miles away in Middle Kentucky, twelve-year-old Preston Taylor was busy growing physically, flourishing intellectually, and maturing spiritually in the environ of chattel enslavement until 1863, when Abraham Lincoln issued the Emancipation Proclamation. This executive order "freed" the 3.2 million enslaved persons in the Confederate states, but did nothing to liberate the 800,000 bondspeople in the border states of Delaware, Kentucky, Maryland, and Missouri. Notwithstanding its limitations, the Emancipation Proclamation did succeed in changing the aim of the Civil War from a conflict to save the Union to a struggle to free the slaves. Equally significant was that Lincoln's Emancipation Proclamation led to the wholesale recruitment of black men into the Union military.[3]

Two months after Abraham Lincoln issued the Emancipation Proclamation, abolitionist Frederick Douglass canvassed western New York to recruit black soldiers for the 54th Massachusetts Regiment being formed in Massachusetts. His two sons, Charles and Lewis, were among the first to enlist. Douglass delineated several reasons why black men should become Union soldiers, declaring: "He who fights the battles of America may claim America as his country—and have that claim respected. Thus in defending your country now against rebels and traitors you are defending your own

---

[2] Ibid.

[3] William C. Harris, *Lincoln and the Border States: Preserving the Union* (Lawrence, KS: University Press of Kansas, 2011), 225. Harris pointed out that Northern politicians agitated for the recruitment of black soldiers because white troops suffered heavy casualties. Eric Foner, *Reconstruction: America's Unfinished Revolution, 1863–1877* (New York: Harper & Row, 1988), 37. Foner observed, "The enlistment of black troops, rather than any act of Kentucky herself, sealed the fate of slavery in the Bluegrass State, but at the war's end more than 65,000 blacks remained in bondage. In fact, slavery did not officially end until the ratification of the Thirteenth Amendment, which, to the last, Kentucky's legislature opposed."

liberty, honor, manhood and self-respect." Furthermore, Douglass viewed the Civil War as a "war for Emancipation," adding:

> The salvation of the country, by the inexorable relation of cause and effect, can be secured only by the complete abolition of Slavery. The President has already proclaimed emancipation to the Slaves in the rebel States which is tantamount to declaring Emancipation in all the States, for Slavery must exist everywhere in the South in order to exist anywhere in the South.[4]

Thirteen-year-old Preston Taylor caught wind of the excitement and opportunity sweeping across black communities in the South. Therefore, in June of 1864, he became one of the 5,405 enslaved men who enlisted in the Union Army at Camp Nelson in Jessamine County, Kentucky. Seven different regiments were organized at Camp Nelson, where Taylor was placed in the 116th United States Colored Troops (116th USCT).[5] This four-year experience in the Union Army forever changed his life, as it polished his literacy and literary skills, shaped his religious convictions, and supplied leadership training skills for all future endeavors.

Taylor without question already possessed some literacy skills, as his biracial status exposed him to opportunities to learn to read and write.[6] Yet, by enrolling in the Union Army, he found ample opportunities to enhance his reading and writing skills. His path intersected at Camp Nelson with John G. Fee, an ardent white abolitionist and educator who arrived at the military post on Independence Day in 1864. A native of Bracken County, Kentucky, Fee grew up in a slaveholding family but converted to the abolitionist

---

[4] Frederick Douglass, "Why Should a Colored Man Enlist?" *Douglass' Monthly* (April 1863); cited in Foner, *Frederick Douglass*, 530. See also, David W. Blight, *Frederick Douglass' Civil War: Keeping Faith in Jubilee* (Baton Rouge, LA: Louisiana State University Press, 1989), 140–174.

[5] Richard D. Sears, *Camp Nelson, Kentucky: A Civil War History* (Lexington, KY: University Press of Kentucky, 2002), xxxix.

[6] S. R. Cassius (1853-1931), an African American leader in the Stone-Campbell movement in Oklahoma, said that he obtained literacy from his mother, Jane, who was taught to read and write by her white mistresses in antebellum Virginia. See Edward J. Robinson, *To Save My Race from Abuse: The Life of Samuel Robert Cassius* (Tuscaloosa, AL: University of Alabama Press, 2007), 1–10. Edward J. Robinson (ed.), *To Lift Up My Race: The Essential Writings of Samuel Robert Cassius* (Knoxville, TN: University of Tennessee Press, 2008), 90.

cause while attending Lane Theological Seminary in Cincinnati, Ohio. Indeed, his conversion to the abolitionist cause was both wholehearted and complete. On one occasion, he recalled witnessing black women tied to trees and whipped with cow-hides on their naked bodies until their "shrieks would seem to rend the very heavens." At another time, he saw a black father, whose only offense was "absenting himself from work for a day and two nights," beaten with a cow-hide on his naked flesh "until his blood ran to his heels."[7]

Such personal encounters with the cruelty and brutality of chattel enslavement propelled Fee into the antislavery movement. "Slavery was a corrupt tree," he asserted, "and bore corrupt fruit,—made many of those who consented to it, not only lawless, but lecherous and vile. Faithful men and women needed to cry out against it."[8] When visiting a black Baptist Church in Kentucky, Fee was moved by the sermon and songs, stating, "I had heard these low wailings before; but a series of experiences, and my situation at that time, all conspired to bring me more fully into sympathy with the sorrowing. I sat and quietly wept—wept with continuous weeping. I was in deep sympathy with burdened spirits."[9]

Driven by an impulse of egalitarianism—the absolute equality between black people and white people on a practical level—Fee vigorously opposed "colonization" schemes to repatriate black people to Africa, insisting that black people possessed the same intelligence and capability as their white counterparts. Racial prejudice, in his view, was a sin based on pride. "Better," he concluded, "that we have black faces than black hearts."[10]

Armed with such strong egalitarian perspectives, Fee arrived at Camp Nelson and immediately began pouring his life and resources into educating and evangelizing African American soldiers, who came to recruiting stations with "cheerful" dispositions and songs of joy. Black enlisted men received bunks, company assignments, uniforms, and weapons. Historian Marion B. Lucas has observed, "Military camp also offered black soldiers an opportunity to improve

---

[7] John G. Fee, *Autobiography of John G. Fee, Berea, Kentucky* (Chicago: National Christian Association, 1891), 69.
[8] Ibid., 116.
[9] Ibid., 143.
[10] Cited in Richard D. Sears, *The Day of Small Things: Abolitionism in the Midst of Slavery, Berea, Kentucky, 1854–1864* (Lanham, MD: University Press of America, 1986), 68.

their minds, bodies, and occasionally their pocketbooks. Many black troops wanted to acquire an education, a desire not ignored by missionary associations."[11]

For Elijah P. Marrs, a former enslaved person who became a sergeant for the 12th Regiment Heavy Artillery United States Colored Troops, the Civil War not only meant his transition from slavery to freedom, it also marked his entry into manhood. When the sergeant called Marrs's name, he answered promptly, adding:

> I can stand this said I, and like a man, with cup, pan, and spoon, marched up to the window and received my rations. It is true I thought of my mother's sweet voice when she used to call me to dine, but "pshaw!" said I, "this is better than slavery, though I do march in line to the tap of the drum." I felt freedom in my bones, and when I saw the American eagle, with outspread wings, upon the American flag, with the motto, "E Pluribus Unum," the thought came to me, "Give me liberty or give me death." Then all fear banished. I had quit thinking as a child and had commenced to think as a man.[12]

The stirring words of Marrs provide a glimpse into the psychology of Preston Taylor and other African American soldiers who enlisted in the Union Army as teenagers but soon matured rapidly. In one sense, regular meals and handsome uniforms appealed to young ex-slaves; in another sense, love of country and freedom molded and inspired their young hearts, imparting lasting virtues of courage and discipline. This was especially true of Taylor.

Moreover, John G. Fee indelibly stamped Taylor and other black soldiers in two significant ways. First, he helped those who were

---

[11] Marion B. Lucas, *A History of Blacks in Kentucky: Volume 1: From Slavery to Segregation, 1760–1891* (Frankfort, KY: Kentucky Historical Society, 1992), 155. Lucas noted, "'Cheerful' recruits, some no more than fifteen years old, journeyed to Louisville to enlist, often having walked long distances. Marching through the streets of Louisville, the new enlistees on one occasion demonstrated their hostility to slavery by singing songs such as 'John Brown.'" The second quote appears on page 169.

[12] Elijah P. Marrs, *Life and History of the Rev. Elijah P. Marrs, First Pastor of Beargrass Baptist Church, and Author* (electronic edition); www.docsouth.unc.edu/neh/marrs; accessed on July 27, 2022. See also Lucas, *A History of Blacks*, 167. After the Civil War, Marrs (1840–1910) emerged as a prominent minister and educator in Kentucky.

either illiterate or quasi-literate to grow and develop their literacy skills. Writing to Simeon S. Jocelyn, a white preacher and abolitionist, Fee expressed optimism:

> I have undertaken to teach the non commissioned officers to read and write. Most of these knew their letters; quite a number could spell a little, and some few could read.—I had no help at first,—now I have the help of one ex-slave—tomorrow one more. The pupils are making astonishing progress, considering the small facilities they have had.—Perhaps no slaves in the nation are superior in intellectual development to these Kentucky exslaves—few their equal.[13]

Fee had been praying for an opportunity to help black people in a substantive way; the work at Camp Nelson was an answer to his prayers. He called it, "'the beginning of the end'—the freedom of men, white and colored; freedom in such manner as would give prestige to the latter, and sympathy from the former."[14] In the post-Civil War world, Taylor would launch his own educational enterprise, perhaps having been inspired by the efforts of Fee.

Second, Fee without question helped to shape Taylor's theological views. In 1855, Fee launched Berea College, free of racism and sectarianism. Board members, wrote Fee, resolved "that Berea College should be under an influence strictly Christian, and, as such, opposed to sectarianism, slave-holding, caste, and every other wrong institution and practice." In Fee's mind, unity was based on Christ. He cited Alexander Campbell, who in his 1837 *Lunenburg Letter*, wrote, "There are Christians among the sects." Fee concluded:

> We then build on Christ, a person, and seek to convert men to him in all the fullness of his character, baptize in his name, gather together for worship and thus constitute the one church of the locality; not as a party, but as a *part of* the whole body of Christ, wearing his name, and his name only.[15]

The influence of Fee's ecumenical views and his interaction with black soldiers of all religious persuasions undoubtedly shaped Taylor's understanding of other faith traditions. A committed

---

[13] Fee to Simeon S. Jocelyn (July 18, 1864); cited in Sears, *Camp Nelson, Kentucky*, 101.
[14] Fee, *Autobiography of John G. Fee*, 175.
[15] Ibid., 40, 185, 207–210.

member of the Stone-Campbell movement, he felt no misgivings about freely mingling and collaborating with African American believers in denominational churches.

Even though Taylor served as a drummer boy in the 116th USCT, there are no known extant sources that detail his military experience at Camp Nelson. Yet Civil War historians attest that drummer boys played a crucial role in the watershed event. They customarily sounded calls on drum, fife, or bugle daily; and they assisted the band in providing music for ceremonies and drills. The private writings of William C. Richardson, a drummer boy for the 104th Ohio Regiment, reveal that, in addition to beating a drum, instrumentalists also carried water for soldiers, sharpened surgeons' utensils, assisted in removing and caring for the wounded, drew maps, and helped bury the dead. Scholar James M. McPherson has explained: "Traditional practice in both armies assigned regimental musicians and soldiers 'least effective under arms' as stretcher-bearers to carry the wounded from the field and assist surgeons in the field hospitals."[16]

Even if drummer boys in the Civil War were in noncombatant positions, that did not mean their duty was without strain or less hazardous. When American Missionary Association (AMA) missionaries William L. and John B. Lowery reached Camp Nelson on August 19, 1864, they expressed disappointment that black soldiers had little time for academics because they had "to drill several hours extra each day."[17] Drummer boys worked just as hard as those who toiled in heavy artillery units. Indeed, William Shakespeare Hays, an American poet, composed the verse, "The Drummer Boy," right after the Battle of Shiloh in 1862. The poem in part reads thus:

> Oh Shiloh's dark and bloody ground, the dead and
>   wounded lay.
> Amongst them was a drummer boy, that beat the drum
>   that day.
> A wounded soldier raised him up, His drum was by
>   his side.

---

[16] Bell Irvin Wiley, *The Life of Billy Yank: The Common Soldier of the Union Army* (New York: Doubleday, 1951/1971), 296. James M. McPherson, *Battle Cry of Freedom: The Civil War Era* (New York: Oxford University Press, 1988), 484.

[17] John B. Lowery to George Whipple (August 27, 1864); cited in Sears, *Camp Nelson, Kentucky*, xiv.

He clasped his hands and raised his eyes and prayed
before he died:

"Look down upon the battle field, Oh Thou,
   our Heav'nly friend,
Have mercy on sinful souls." The soldiers cried, "Amen."
For gather'd round a little group, Each brave man knelt
   and cried.
They listened to the drummer boy who prayed before
he died.[18]

This emotional poem reveals the attachment and affection that soldiers had for drummer boys; more importantly, it shows the dangers to which even musicians found themselves exposed.

Preston Taylor's regiment, the 116th USCT, took part in the siege of Petersburg, Virginia, which lasted from around October 1, 1864 to March 25, 1865. Ulysses S. Grant and Union forces weakened the Petersburg defenses and captured an important fort only six miles from Richmond, Virginia. African American soldiers, consisting of three divisions, "tasted here their first combat and performed well." The siege of Petersburg ultimately resulted in a Union victory, subsequently leading to the capture of Richmond, the capital of the Confederacy. Civil War expert James McPherson described the import of the siege of Petersburg this way: "As Jefferson Davis worshipped at St. Paul Church in Richmond this balmy Sunday, a messenger tiptoed down the aisle and gave him a telegram. It was from Lee: Richmond must be given up. Turning pale, the president left the church without a word."[19]

The fall of Richmond all but signaled the end of the Civil War and a Union victory. After Union soldiers departed Richmond, mobs came out at night and set the city ablaze. "Southerners burned more of their own capital than the enemy had burned of Atlanta or Columbia." Yankee soldiers accompanied by black troops returned to help extinguish the flames. Indeed, black residents in Richmond welcomed and returned thanks for Union troops for the

---

[18] William Shakespeare Hays, "The Drummer Boy of Shiloh," in Henry Steele Commanger (ed.), *The Civil War Archive: The History of the Civil War in Documents* (New York: Black Dog & Leventhal Publishers, 1950/2000), 394–395.

[19] McPherson, *Battle Cry of Freedom*, 740, 846.

emancipation of "their race." And when President Abraham Lincoln visited the city of Richmond on April 4, 1865, African American locals shouted, "Glory! Glory! Glory!" Civil War historian Richard Wheeler observed, "Their deliverer had come—he who, next to the Lord Jesus, was their best friend! It was not a hurrah that they gave so much as a wild, jubilant cry of inexpressible joy."[20] Shortly after the surrender of Richmond, Robert E. Lee met Ulysses S. Grant at the Appomattox Courthouse, thus officially ending the Civil War.[21] As a drummer boy in the 116th USCT, Preston Taylor witnessed all of these pivotal events and performed some key roles in them.

Taylor never forgot these experiences of his teenage years. Indeed, seventeen years after the Civil War, he traveled from Mt. Sterling, Kentucky, to Richmond, Virginia, and reminisced: "We passed the Episcopal church where Jefferson Davis was worshiping when he received the telegram of the surrender of General Lee."[22] Pivotal events from the war lingered in his mind and indelibly molded his character and career. Furthermore, the constant drilling and disciplined regimen he received in the United States military without doubt permanently stamped his life, propelling him forward in the postwar world with deep religious convictions, intellectual acumen, leadership skills, and ecumenical perspectives. Such exceptional qualities prepared him to assume influential roles in the Stone-Campbell movement and in the broader American context. Equally significant, as a drummer boy and a stretcher-bearer on the Civil War battlefield, Taylor saw death and carnage firsthand—all of which prepared him for his future occupations as a minister and undertaker among African Americans in Middle Tennessee and beyond.

---

[20] Richard Wheeler, *Witness to Appomattox* (New York: Harper & Row, 1989), 105–107, 129.
[21] McPherson, *Battle Cry of Freedom*, 740, 846.
[22] Preston Taylor, "Our Colored Brethren," *Christian Standard* 17 (October 21, 1882): 336.

Part 2

Successes and Struggles in Kentucky, 1870-1884

Three

'His Highest Calling'

The Polity and Theology of Preston Taylor

Preach the word; be instant in season, out of season; reprove, rebuke, exhort with all long suffering and doctrine.
—2 Timothy 4:2

The Christian life is an upward journey, as well as a straight one, and each one should try to please his Master in all things, knowing he holds his life in his hand and will reward each one for his faithfulness. —Preston Taylor

When the Civil War ended in 1865, African Americans in Kentucky faced what one scholar has called "freedom's pains."[1] The abolition of chattel enslavement and the ratification of the Thirteenth Amendment failed to eradicate white racism. Racial discrimination against black Kentuckians manifested itself in various ways. Restricted mobility and mob violence combined to keep black freed people in a state of subservience. The Freedmen's Bureau, designed to assist African Americans transitioning from bondage to freedom, reported for 1867-1868 that twenty-six black residents in Kentucky were murdered among the 327 incidents of abuse and violence.[2] In his insightful study on African Americans in Louisville, Kentucky, historian George C. Wright noted, "White

---
[1] Marion B. Lucas, *A History of Blacks in Kentucky, Volume 1: From Slavery to Segregation* (Frankfort, KY: Kentucky Historical Society, 1992), 178.
[2] Ibid., 188-189.

hostility was always present, often working effectively to negate black gains."[3]

In spite of facing stiff opposition, black Kentuckians found glimmers of hope in the post-Civil War world. Northern philanthropists and black self-help groups collaborated to address the needs of impoverished freedmen. Several months after the Civil War's end, black residents in Paducah, Kentucky, organized a Freedmen's Aid Society. In the winter of 1866, the Fifth Street Baptist Church in Louisville launched a movement for a hospital for African Americans. The following spring, a Freedmen's Sanitary Commission grew out of a concerned citizens meeting in the same city.[4] Virtually abandoned by the federal government and viciously harassed by white terrorist groups, African Americans in Kentucky found strength in God and in one another.

Preston Taylor, a member of the 116th USCT Regiment, ushered out of the military into this complex world mixed with shadows of gloom and flashes of sunlight. In 1870, he was one of 222,210 black residents living in Kentucky; a decade later, he was among 271,451 black inhabitants there.[5] Like many fellow black Kentuckians, Taylor imbibed a spirit of grit and determination. As scholars John Hope Franklin and Evelyn Brooks Higginbotham have argued:

> Bombarded with persuasive representations of black inferiority in the white press, the legal system, the consumer economy, science, popular culture, and many other daily reminders of the "Negro's place" in society, black people embraced the ideology of self-help as one way of reaffirming their personal dignity and their hope for a better future for themselves and their children.[6]

Building on his military experience in the Union military, Taylor emerged in postbellum Kentucky as a spiritual leader, pouring

---

[3] George C. Wright, *Life Behind a Veil: Blacks in Louisville, Kentucky, 1865–1930* (Baton Rouge, LA: Louisiana State University Press, 1985), 38.

[4] Lucas, *A History*, 185, 200. James D. Anderson, *The Education of Blacks in the South, 1860–1935* (Chapel Hill, NC: University of North Carolina Press, 1988), 13. Anderson has noted that in post–Civil War Kentucky, houses of worship also functioned as "school houses in the South."

[5] Lucas, *A History*, 179.

[6] John Hope Franklin and Evelyn Brooks Higginbotham, *From Slavery to Freedom: A History of African Americans* (9th ed.) (New York: McGraw-Hill, 2011), 288.

his efforts into three areas: the railroad industry, educational enterprises, and congregational ministry. Most black railroaders toiled as cooks, waiters, and porters. As a porter on the L & C (Louisville and Chattanooga) Railroad, Taylor carried bags, shined shoes, ironed clothes, and brought food to patrons. The railroad industry offered African Americans "real, if limited," opportunities.[7]

Postbellum newspapers across the South often portrayed black freedmen as murderers and thieves.[8] A correspondent from Frankfort, Kentucky, wrote,

> Complaints are coming up here from all quarters that negroes are destroying all the fish in the rivers, creeks, and ponds, by their incessant seining, dipping, and other unfair modes of taking them. I am assured by one gentleman who is posted on the subject, that these lazy creatures lounge about the locks and dams and take every fine fish that comes up on the way to its spawning ground.[9]

As a railroad worker, Taylor set out to refute such racist caricatures with physical toil and exertion. In the 1870s, African American railroad workers in Kentucky accused white contractors of biasedly excluding them from work and wage-earning opportunities. Upon learning about the allegations, Taylor immediately intervened in the dispute and offered to build two sections of the Chesapeake and Ohio Railroad with black laborers. After receiving the contract, he assembled a labor force of 150 black men with seventy-five horses, mules, carts, and wagons. Taylor "led the way," as he and his cohorts completed the contract ahead of schedule.[10]

The impressive feat of Taylor and his black army prompted Collis P. Huntington, a premier railroad industrialist, to exclaim, "I have built thousands of miles of road but I never before saw a contractor who finished his contract in advance."[11] Huntington sympathized with the plight of African Americans, supported Booker T. Washington's

---

[7] Eric Arnesen, *Brotherhoods of Color: Black Railroad Workers and the Struggle for Equality* (Cambridge, MA: Harvard University Press, 2001), 24.

[8] "Southern Items," *Louisville Daily Courier* (January 18, 1867): 3; "Southern Items," *Louisville Daily Courier* (January 21, 1867): 2.

[9] "From Frankfort," *Louisville Daily Courier* (February 2, 1867): 1.

[10] William J. Simmons, *Men of Mark: Eminent, Progressive, and Rising* (New York: Arno Press, 2887/1968), 298. Lucas, *A History*, 278.

[11] Simmons, *Men of Mark*, 298.

Tuskegee Institute, and urged railroad superintendents in the South to employ black workers.[12] Taylor's accomplishment stirred a national publication to call him a man desirous of opening doors of opportunity for black people.[13]

Taylor's occupation as a porter and construction worker on the railroad helped to mold his character and to sharpen his leadership skills. He was a man who fought racist stereotypes circulating about black people in the national media while simultaneously championing the cause of racial justice and economic equality for his people in the labor force and beyond.

The New Castle Bible School

After the Civil War, educational institutions for black people sprang up across the South because of the desire of African Americans to learn and the commitment of white Northern missionaries to teach. Various religious groups—such as Baptists, Methodists, and Presbyterians—pooled their resources to launch colleges and universities for black freed people. As historians John Hope Franklin and Evelyn Brooks Higginbotham observed:

> The American Missionary Society, and the societies of the Baptists, Methodists, Presbyterians, and Episcopalians, were all active in establishing schools, and by 1867 schools had been set up in counties throughout the former Confederacy. Two years later nearly 3,000 schools, serving over 150,000 pupils, reported to the bureau, the supervision of which monopolized much of the agents' time.[14]

White adherents of the Stone-Campbell movement refused to be left behind by their white religious neighbors. In 1873, Winthrop

---

[12] David Lavender, *The Great Persuader* (Niwot, CO: University Press of Colorado, 1969/1998), 350–351. Stephen E. Ambrose, *Nothing Like It in the World: The Men Who Built the Transcontinental Railroad, 1863–1869* (New York Simon & Schuster, 2000), 243. Ambrose observed that Collis P. Huntington (1821–1900) also favored using Chinese laborers to build railroads out West. For more information on the significance of Huntington, see Michael Hiltzik, *Iron Empires: Robber Barons, Railroads, and the Making of Modern America* (Boston: Mariner Books, 2021), 183, 245–246, 252–253, 255.

[13] Clement Richardson (ed.), *The National Cyclopedia of the Colored Race* (Montgomery, AL: National Publishing, 1919), 334.

[14] Franklin and Higginbotham, *From Slavery to Freedom*, 250.

H. Hopson—an influential preacher in Louisville, Kentucky, and a former chaplain for the Confederate Army—raised funds to organize the Louisville Bible School. The academy lasted only three years and had just ten to twelve students, but it yielded impressive fruit. H. Jackson Brayboy, an African American preacher, studied at the Louisville Bible School and engaged in effective evangelistic preaching in Alabama.[15]

In the early 1880s, Taylor revived the Louisville Bible School, relocated it to New Castle, Kentucky, and renamed it New Castle Bible School. The Christian Women's Board of Missions, formed in 1874, cast its full support behind Taylor as "financial agent of the New Castle School."[16] In spite of reports that the school had several teachers and a "bright future,"[17] and despite his success in raising $2,200, the New Castle Bible School failed. The Board of Negro Education and Evangelization in 1891 attributed the collapse to being "badly located and badly managed. This institution received its buildings from the contributions of Kentucky Disciples, and it was partly sustained by financial help from the State Mission Board."[18]

Even though the foregoing "obituary" cited poor management and inadequate monetary support, there were no doubt other factors that contributed to the failure of the New Castle Bible School. The emergence of other Stone-Campbell institutions—such as the Southern Christian Institute (1882) in Edwards, Mississippi, the Lum Grade School (1894) in Lum, Alabama, and S. R. Cassius's Tohee Industrial School (1898) in Tohee, Oklahoma[19]—competed for black students and diluted donations from white Christians.

Additionally, Taylor stretched himself too thin, juggling multiple responsibilities in various places. His work as porter on the railroad took him away from his pastoral ministry in Mt. Sterling, Kentucky; and these duties consumed large chunks of his time and thwarted his fundraising efforts for the New Castle Bible School. Shuffling numerous projects and obligations perhaps contributed to two failed

---

[15] David Edwin Harrell, Jr., *Sources of Division in the Disciples of Christ, 1865–1900: A Social History of the Disciples of Christ, Volume 2* (Tuscaloosa, AL: University of Alabama Press, 1973/2003), 185.
[16] Ibid., 194.
[17] Simmons, *Men of Mark*, 298.
[18] Cited in Harrell, *Sources of Division*, 194.
[19] Edward J. Robinson, *To Save My Race from Abuse: The Life of Samuel Robert Cassius* (Tuscaloosa, AL: University of Alabama Press, 2007).

marriages in Kentucky. Court documents show that in 1870 Taylor united in marriage to Ellen (or Ella) Spradling, but by decade's end, the union had dissolved. In 1880, he married Anna Hoffman; this marriage also unraveled (see Chapter 4 for more information). I am unsure what actually ended his marriages in Kentucky, yet maybe the virtues of "nerve and iron-will" that led to his ecclesiastical and entrepreneurial successes proved to be vices of stubbornness and overcommitment that troubled his personal life.

Pastoral Ministry in Kentucky

In post–Civil War Kentucky, Taylor toiled as a champion of higher education for African Americans and a porter on the railroad. But he was much more. Esteemed educator Booker T. Washington bestowed lofty praise on Taylor, noting, "He has interested himself along other lines; but not for a single year since arriving at maturity has he neglected what he regarded as his highest calling."[20] Taylor's "highest calling" was preaching and pastoring his people in the Bluegrass State.

From 1871 to 1885, Taylor shepherded a Christian Church in Mt. Sterling, Kentucky; while there, he helped to organize a congregation in Millersburg, Kentucky, and he continued to minister to congregations in the Mid-South and beyond. His evangelistic zeal impressed author and educator William J. Simmons, who boasted that Taylor succeeded in "building up the largest congregation in the State among his faith, besides building them the finest brick edifice, as a place for the worship of God, in that section of the State."[21]

But Preston Taylor was a practical theologian, in that he reached beyond the pulpit to comfort the afflicted and oppressed. In the spring of 1879, he testified to visiting prisoners in the Montgomery County, Kentucky, jail, stating:

> Among the tombs and in the cold and dark cages of the prison we have found our way quite frequently, in our county jail, here of late, to administer to the sick and troubled. We found they needed prayer, and by their cordial

---

[20] Booker T. Washington, *The Negro in Business* (New York: AMS Press, 1907/1971), 100.

[21] Simmons, *Men of Mark*, 297. See also, Hap Lyda, "A History of Black Christian Churches (Disciples of Christ) in the United States through 1899" (PhD diss., Vanderbilt University, 1972), 40.

invitation, last Lord's day, accompanied by some twelve or fifteen members of the church, we consented to be locked up with them, and then we raised our songs and prayers to God, and preached to them on the subject of Peace. He based his sermon on Jesus's statement in Matthew 5:9, "Blessed are the peacemakers: for they shall be called the children of God." Perhaps because of his own experience as a formerly enslaved youth, Taylor expressed sympathy and empathy toward those incarcerated. "No one can appreciate freedom and liberty so highly," he lamented, "as one who is somewhat acquainted with the prisoner's life." He then urged his *Christian Standard* readers to ponder seriously the Lord's words in Matthew 25:36, adding: "Visit the jail of your county, and get a blessing." Four years later, he reported that African American Disciples in Kentucky had 4,216 adherents, yielded 251 baptisms, and raised $85,000—far exceeding fellow black Disciples in North Carolina, Mississippi, Tennessee, Ohio, Indiana, Missouri, and Kansas.[22]

Taylor, however, ascended to national prominence in the Stone-Campbell movement in 1879, when he became editor of "Our Colored Brethren," a column in the *Christian Standard*, a religious paper established by Isaac Errett thirteen years earlier. Taylor's small section offers huge and insightful glimpses into the congregational activity and theological formation of African American Disciples of Christ. Indeed, Stephen Dawson, a church leader in Roaring Spring, Kentucky, said that, although he had heard of Taylor for years, "yet never seen you, I feel that I know you." Through the pages of Errett's paper, the black evangelist became a household name. In the early 1880s, the *Christian Standard* boasted a readership of more than 50,000.

Juggling preaching and writing responsibilities, however, proved no easy chore. Indeed, in the winter of 1882, Taylor accidentally left

---

[22] For Preston Taylor's visit to jail in Montgomery County, Kentucky, see Taylor, "Our Colored Brethren," *Christian Standard* 16 (April 26, 1879): 133. Preston Taylor, "Our Colored Brethren," *Christian Standard* 17 (December 23, 1882): 425. Taylor never used the phrase, "social gospel," yet he believed in serving people "outside the walls" of the church building. For a succinct and insightful treatment of the "social gospel" in African American Churches, see Anthony B. Pinn, *Introducing African American Religion* (New York: Routledge, 2013), 180–183.

his mailbox key at the Post Office, and a mischievous youth got hold of it, causing some of his correspondence to be lost. He reported an eleven-year-old boy "robbed me of my mails for a week before it was discovered, and when the detective caught him he had in his possession several of my letters, and others he had torn into fragments. Any one whose articles do not receive attention, or any letter unanswered, please notify me at once."[23] Notwithstanding this mishap, Taylor generally handled correspondence from fellow black Disciples responsibly.

The "Our Colored Brethren" column shows that Taylor performed weddings for young couples. On February 24, 1881, he married Crawford Boyd and Annie Jones; a few weeks later, he united in holy matrimony William Jowett and Martha Todd.[24] He also conducted many funerals during his ministerial tenure at Mt. Sterling. He lauded Sister Clary Warfield as a "faithful soldier of Jesus for twenty years, and was one of the most consecrated I ever knew," adding, "She was a Joshua in speech, 'As for me and my house, we will serve the Lord.'"[25] The Mt. Sterling congregation lost Sister Margaret Whaley, who was "rich in good works," and Sister Ann Coleman, a "disciple of Jesus" and an "earnest Christian."[26] After Sister Bettie Johnson passed away, an exasperated preacher expressed relief: "This makes 7 who we consider among the best of members, lost out of this congregation this year; but we are thankful to report all are well now."[27]

The Mt. Sterling Christian Church, however, gained more members than they lost. Unlike some black Disciple congregations that met sporadically, the Mt. Sterling flock gathered for fellowship and heard preaching each week. Consequently, Taylor proudly reported many "additions." On September 8, 1882, he announced

---

[23] Stephen Dawson, "Our Colored Brethren," *Christian Standard* 14 (September 27, 1879): 309. J. C. Graves, "Our Colored Brethren," *Christian Standard* 17 (September 9, 1882): 288. For the account of Preston Taylor's mail being lost and stolen, see Taylor, "Our Colored Brethren," *Christian Standard* 17 (March 4, 1882): 69.

[24] Preston Taylor, "Our Colored Brethren," *Christian Standard* 16 (March 12, 1881): 93.

[25] Ibid.

[26] Preston Taylor, "Our Colored Brethren," *Christian Standard* 16 (March 26, 1881): 101. Preston Taylor, "Our Colored Brethren," *Christian Standard* 16 (May 21, 1881): 165.

[27] Preston Taylor, "Our Colored Brethren," *Christian Standard* 16 (June 11, 1881): 189.

five additions, one from the Baptists, one from the Methodists, and three by letters, adding, "Many were turned back from want of seating capacity."[28] Three months later, a protracted meeting with preaching from M. F. Robinson, Green Clay Smith, and W. H. Brown yielded "23 accessions."[29] Even though Taylor and other men helped to build the Mt. Sterling congregation, women played a significant role as well. Pastor Taylor announced the Ladies' Association of Mt. Sterling had raised $50 on Independence Day to "carpet the church."[30] Two months later, the Mt. Sterling fellowship had one baptism and raised $150.[31] The same congregation led the way in giving funds to establish a black Christian Church in Washington, D.C.[32]

African American Disciples, through Preston Taylor's column, displayed their interest in education. In 1881, Berea College, established by abolitionist John G. Fee twenty-six years earlier, reported a total enrollment of 369 students, with 203 male students and 163 female students.[33] When the Southern Christian Institute opened its doors in Mississippi in the same year, the Taylor column happily announced an enrollment of 100 students, while pleading, "Do not let this school fall to the ground, as the one at Louisville did, and ruin our progress."[34]

Taylor's "Our Colored Brethren" section also incorporated political happenings. After James A. Garfield entered the White House as the twentieth president of the United States on March 4, 1881, Taylor prayed to God "to remember kindly our brother, Jas. A. Garfield."[35] Six months later, when Mr. Garfield was tragically

---

[28] Preston Taylor, "Our Colored Brethren," *Christian Standard* 17 (September 23, 1882): 299.

[29] Preston Taylor, "Our Colored Brethren," *Christian Standard* 17 (December 16, 1882): 413.

[30] Preston Taylor, "Our Colored Brethren," *Christian Standard* 17 (July 15, 1882): 219.

[31] Preston Taylor, "Our Colored Brethren," *Christian Standard* 17 (September 30, 1882): 309.

[32] Preston Taylor, "Our Colored Brethren," *Christian Standard* 16 (November 19, 1881): 373. Preston Taylor, "Our Colored Brethren," *Christian Standard* 16 (November 26, 1881): 381.

[33] Preston Taylor, "Our Colored Brethren," *Christian Standard* 16 (February 5, 1881): 48.

[34] Preston Taylor, "Our Colored Brethren," *Christian Standard* 16 (March 12, 1881): 88.

[35] Ibid.

assassinated, the Mt. Sterling minister noted, "Our beloved President Garfield was not forgotten in the service of the day."[36]

Polity, Theology, and African American Disciples

As editor of the "Our Colored Brethren" column, Preston Taylor weighed in on various issues, including instrumental music in worship, denominational churches, false preachers, and baptism. When discussing the matter of the "organ in the church," he urged that "we must not let these minor questions impede our pursuit after godliness." The Mt. Sterling preacher viewed the use of instruments in worship as a personal preference, and because of congregational autonomy, he argued that each local church should decide for themselves. He added,

> One congregation may use the organ, and another may oppose it, and this is because we are human, and can't all think alike. The matter is one of the untaught problems of the Bible, and expediency must govern the case, and the peace of God which passeth all understanding shall keep your hearts and minds through Christ Jesus.[37]

Reflecting the influence that *The Last Will and Testament of the Springfield Presbytery* had on his theological understanding,[38] he excoriated Methodist leaders who called themselves reverend, elder, bishop, doctor of divinity, "and many such plastered names for fame."[39] He also chided preachers who neglected the "old story of Jesus and Him crucified," while seeking to "satisfy itching ears." He lamented,

> We are often asked why hundreds and thousands do not join the church now, as they did in the apostolic times. It does not take the eye of an angel to see why they do not: because the way of preaching the gospel has become so perverted, that

---

[36] Preston Taylor, "Our Colored Brethren," 16 *Christian Standard* (October 22, 1881): 341.

[37] Preston Taylor, "Our Colored Brethren," 16 (January 8, 1881): 13

[38] In 1804, Barton W. Stone issued *The Last Will and Testament of the Springfield Presbytery* and rejected the use of lofty titles such as "Reverend."

[39] Preston Taylor, "Our Colored Brethren," *Christian Standard* 16 (January 15, 1881): 21. Ironically, Taylor was often addressed as "Reverend," and he himself consistently wore the designation "Elder" during his ministerial tenure in Nashville, Tennessee.

among the hundreds of pulpits occupied few are arsenals of salvation to a world of wickedness.[40]

A pivotal tenet of Alexander Campbell was the mode and design of baptism, which he first declared openly in his 1823 debate with Presbyterian minister William Maccalla. In the summer of 1881, Taylor reprinted a poem read by Annie Frazier before the Danville, Kentucky, Christian Sunday School Convention. It read in part:

Buried by baptism, interred,
That is the meaning of the Word.
Such is the language of our version.
And looks a great deal like immersion.[41]

The poem specifically refutes the position of Methodists, who practiced sprinkling for immersion, and other religious groups who downplayed the importance of baptism.

On January 2, 1881, thirty-two-year-old Preston Taylor preached a sermon titled, "Death and Life," at the High Street Christian Church in Mt. Sterling, and he republished it in his edited column. The homily reveals his eschatological views about life after death. Lifting his text from Colossians 3:3, the preacher couched his Christology in economic language. "Christ is your treasurer," he proclaimed, "and we commit our souls to him as to a faithful curator that is able to keep us against the day of his coming. We have long adopted this bank as the most suitable depository for our money."[42]

After having survived a brutal Civil War and having conducted many funerals, Taylor explained that death is a separation of the soul and body. The body goes to the grave, and the soul departs to God:

---

[40] Preston Taylor, "Our Colored Brethren," *Christian Standard* 16 (January 22, 1881): 29.

[41] Annie Fraizer, "Our Colored Brethren," *Christian Standard* 16 (August 6, 1881): 253. So also, Benjamin King, a noteworthy black preacher in Ohio, who listed several scriptures—including Mark 1:4-5; Luke 3:3; and Acts 2:38; 22:16—to emphasize that baptism was for the remission of sins. Benjamin King, "Our Colored Brethren," *Christian Standard* 17 (November 18, 1882): 365. For a useful discussion of the Campbell–Maccalla debate, see Leroy Garrett, *The Stone-Campbell Movement: The Story of the American Restoration Movement* (Joplin, MO: College Press, 1981/2006), 134–135.

[42] Preston Taylor, "Our Colored Brethren," *Christian Standard* 16 (February 12, 1881): 53.

> [Death is the] sentence passed by the judge upon the exiles from paradise; but inasmuch as we all die in Adam, we are made alive in Christ; but not until we die with him; for no one in the flesh can please God, that is, fleshy minded—and to abolish worldly mind, we must be transformed by the renewing of our minds by the Holy Spirit.[43]

This was a fusion of Romans 5, Romans 8, and 1 Corinthians 15, which Taylor appropriated to tell his listeners: "You are in the world but not of the world. We have been separated from our relation to the world by our death to it."[44] His Christological, eschatological, and pneumatological understandings furnished the foundation for moral Christian behavior. He expounded:

> The Christian life is an upward journey, as well as a straight one, and each one should try to please his Master in all things, knowing he holds his life in his hand and will reward each one for his faithfulness. One of the most encouraging things about our Savior is, he does not task his people to greater work than they are able to perform; but he is willing to accept of the best we do for him.[45]

In the mind of Preston Taylor, the Christian life was a victorious life, a life that propelled people—even and especially black people—upward and onward morally and spiritually.

D. R. Wilkins

Knowing that there were many talented black preachers in his chosen fellowship, Taylor often published sermon excerpts of fellow ministers in the "Our Colored Brethren" column. In the spring of 1881, D. R. Wilkins, pastor of the Second Christian Church in Paducah, Kentucky, delivered a sermon titled, "The Prodigal Son." Working from Luke 15:11–32, Wilkins delineated ten points.

1. the free agency of man;
2. that man sins of his own choice;
3. the joy which sin gives for a short season;
4. the want to which sin is sure to reduce one;
5. the association to which sin necessarily brings the person who follows it;

---
[43] Ibid.
[44] Ibid.
[45] Ibid.

6. we get here a practical explanation as to what repentance is;
7. that the sinner is to approach God with all his sins;
8. that God is willing to welcome all who come to him by faith;
9. that there is a great joy among the righteous at the return of sinners to God; and
10. that we who are enjoying the blessings of God's spiritual kingdom should not become envious of the blessings bestowed on our less fortunate brother.

Wilkins concluded his discourse: "All were happy except the elder brother, and all was his, but he murmured. Beloved, let us be content with what we get of the sweets of heaven and not get out of sorts because God is good and helps others."[46]

Like many of their white counterparts in the Stone-Campbell movement, Wilkins and other African American Disciples of Christ espoused an Arminian view of salvation—namely, that man has the power to accept or reject the gift of forgiveness. The prodigal chose to sin and subsequently chose to repent and return to God "with all his sins." Wilkins's sermon communicated a gospel of grace and mercy. While some white and black Stone-Campbell adherents preached a "hard"[47] and merciless message, others like Wilkins stood on a gospel of love and grace.

J. C. Graves

J. C. Graves surfaced as another gifted black preacher in Taylor's column. Samuel Buckner, an African American preacher in Germantown, Kentucky, reported that "J. C. Graves did the best piece of work of his life; sixteen additions."[48] Graves pastored a Christian Church in Paris, Kentucky, where he gave a homily titled, "Unexpected Good." He emphasized God's track record of bringing good out of evil, as seen in the lives of Joseph, Jesus, and Paul, noting,

> The people had classed Nazareth with the worst places on earth, so much so that when the prophet said that God would

---

[46] D. R. Wilkins, "Our Colored Brethren," *Christian Standard* 16 (May 21, 1881): 165.

[47] Richard T. Hughes, *Reviving the Ancient Faith: The Story of Churches of Christ* (Abilene, TX: Abilene Christian University Press, 1996/2008), 47–91.

[48] Samuel Buckner, "Our Colored Brethren," *Christian Standard* 17 (June 3, 1882): 171.

call his Son out of Nazareth, they say, "Can any good come out of Nazareth?" Yet against their conclusions and expectation, the Saviour of the world came right from the place where they thought nothing good could possibly come.[49]

He then pointed to Saul the persecutor: "Among all the persecutors of the Christian Church 'Paul was chief, but out of that evil comes our chief apostle.'" Graves pointed to Jesus and Paul to allay his listeners' fear of death, stating, "We all dread death, but think of the glorious resurrection—to be with and like Christ—and the fear vanishes."[50]

Graves also possessed a fiery and feisty demeanor in his preaching and teaching. In the fall of 1881, he debated James Thomas, a Baptist clergyman. Thomas argued, "The Baptist Church is the Church of Christ," but Graves denied the proposition. H. M. Ayers, a preacher for a Christian Church in Lexington and the debate's moderator, reported that Thomas failed to "throw any light" on the subject and accused Graves of belonging to the "Campbellite Church, and A. Campbell was Elder Graves' father." Graves then questioned Thomas: Can one be a member of the Baptist Church "without being baptized?" The latter replied emphatically: No! The former retorted, "[T]hen a man can get to heaven and not be a member of the Baptist Church—according to your own words, as you say he can get to heaven and not be baptized, but he can not be a member of the Baptist Church unless he is baptized." Graves concluded, "[A] man need not join a Baptist Church; so the Baptist Church cannot be the Church of Christ, because he must be a member of the Church of Christ to get to heaven."[51]

Graves's argument stirred the ire of Thomas, who thanked God that he had seen "Baptists die shouting and praising the Lord." The latter's comments made his supporters at the debate shout, and "made Thomas very glad indeed." The debate's referee noted that Graves had him [Thomas] in a "hard place, when he made him say a man need not join the Baptist Church to get to heaven. ... Very hard on the reverend gentleman."

---

[49] J. C. Graves, "Our Colored Brethren," *Christian Standard* 16 (April 30, 1881): 144.
[50] Ibid.
[51] H. M. Ayers, "Our Colored Brethren," *Christian Standard* 17 (May 20, 1882): 155.

Ayers then concluded, "J. C. Graves is a close debater. Don't forget he is a strong young man—I mean strong in mind, good head."[52] The foregoing exchange is indeed instructive for three reasons. First, it opens a window into the polity and theology of black Disciples in the late nineteenth century. African Americans in the Stone-Campbell movement followed in the debating tradition of one of their principal leaders, Alexander Campbell, who engaged in several major debates.[53] Second, the sermons of Preston Taylor and D. R. Wilkins, coupled with the debating skills of J. C. Graves, attest that the movement of black Disciples of Christ was rife with skilled preachers and talented evangelists, who possessed a combative edge and an exclustivistic posture. The Thomas–Graves debate reveals that the latter, along with other black people of his faith tradition, believed that a "man must be a member of the Church of Christ to get to heaven."[54]

In addition, that Taylor included the discussion between Thomas and Graves in his edited column clearly discloses his theological leanings and perspectives. It seems that the Preston Taylor of Kentucky differed greatly from the Preston Taylor of Nashville, Tennessee. The former was a rising, struggling, and burgeoning churchman; the latter became a prosperous entrepreneur and a renowned civic and church leader. Just as the Alexander Campbell of the *Christian Baptist* was exclusivistic, iconoclastic, and rigid in his theological understanding, but later became more open and cordial toward his religious neighbors, a similar transformation happened to Taylor. The pastor in Mt. Sterling, Kentucky, appeared to be harsh and hard toward his religious neighbors, but Taylor the bank executive, funeral director, mason, and minister in Nashville freely mingled with Baptists, Methodists, and other black religionists. He preached in their churches, and they delivered sermons in his pulpit.

---

[52] Ibid.

[53] See Douglas A. Foster, Newell D. Williams, Paul Blowers, and Anthony Dunnavant (eds.), *The Encyclopedia of the Stone-Campbell Movement* (Grand Rapids, MI: Eerdmans, 2004). See also Bill Humble, *Campbell and Controversy: The Story of Alexander Campbell's Five Great Debates with Skepticism, Catholicism, and Presbyterianism* (Joplin, MO: College Press, 1986). Richard J. Cherok, *Debating for God: Alexander Campbell's Challenge to Skepticism in Antebellum America* (Abilene, TX: Abilene Christian University Press, 2008).

[54] H. M. Ayers, "Our Colored Brethren," *Christian Standard* 17 (May 20, 1882): 155.

H. S. Berry, Sr.

"Honor to whom honor is due" were the words Taylor lavished upon H. S. Berry, Sr., preaching minister for the Gay Street Christian Church in Nashville, Tennessee. After praising Berry and his wife, Taylor expressed gratitude that "God has blessed him with a son, and his name is H. S. Berry, Jr.," adding, "May he be, as Brother and Sister Berry have been, faithful workers in the cause of the Master; and when their heads are grown old, may he come in with vigor to preach the word."[55]

The elder Berry was a frequent contributor to the *Christian Standard* and a well-known itinerant preacher across the Mid-South, even though his home congregation was in Middle Tennessee. In the spring of 1880, he declared to *Christian Standard* readers, "Tennessee has begun to 'awake out of sleep and arise from the dead, that Christ may give them light.' They have caught the missionary spirit, and will hold two district conventions soon" at Little Rock and Bristol, Tennessee.[56] Berry enjoyed camaraderie with other black Disciples preachers. After noting that M. F. Womack had relocated to Dickson, Tennessee, while teaching school and running a grocery store, Berry offered a mixture of praise and a mild rebuke: "Go on, my brother, and after a while I hope you may be able to do more for the Master by devoting your life to his noble causes." In the same article, he acknowledged that S. W. Womack, M. F. Womack's brother, was busy organizing the forthcoming district convention and "desires a large delegation."[57]

In the first week of May, Berry closed a month-long meeting for Taylor and the High Street Christian Church in Mt. Sterling, Kentucky. Taylor commended the guest evangelist:

> Bro. H. S. Berry proved to be *the man* for the meeting. His sermons were well selected and adapted to the occasion, and the greatest of all, they were not delivered in vain, but God opened the hearts of many who accepted of the call and became obedient to the faith.

---

[55] Preston Taylor, "Our Colored Brethren," *Christian Standard* 14 (December 27, 1879): 413.

[56] H. S. Berry, "Our Colored Brethren," *Christian Standard* 15 (April 17, 1880): 125.

[57] H. S. Berry, "Our Colored Brethren," *Christian Standard* 15 (May 1, 1880): 141.

He then reported twenty-seven seekers were "enrolled on our books," thirteen of whom confessed Christ and received baptism. Taylor then boasted, "None have a better church in the city, and our future is flattering."[58]

A competent and zealous churchman, Berry preached sermons to the Gay Street saints, and he contributed articles to the *Christian Standard* to encourage fellow Christians to pursue higher moral ground. He exhorted,

> Brethren, let us all begin to labor to bring ourselves and our congregations to a higher standard of Christian duty, that the world may see our good works and be constrained to glorify our Father which is in heaven and when the day shall dawn that brings time to an end, the sun cease its shining, the moon to give her light, and the stars withdraw their silvery ... we can say, as Paul did, I am ready; I have kept the faith.[59]

In addition to being an exhorter, Berry possessed an abrasive personality. When traveling and preaching in Ohio, he commended the work of Benjamin King, a "man who works with a zeal rarely surpassed." He then rebuked W. H. Brown, a former member and preacher for the Christian Church and an alumnus of the Louisville Bible School, who "found the only *true* light of truth—in the A. M. E. Church—where he now preaches the faith he once destroyed." Brown explained that his reason for leaving the Christian Church was this: "The Methodists pay more money than do the Christians." Berry then assailed Brown, stating, "*Filthy lucre* is all he seems to want." After citing a line from the Roman poet Virgil, Berry concluded, "We wish him no harm in his new espousals, but offer a slight warning to be cautious in his great eagerness to get riches, lest the word be choked and be become unfruitful; better esteem reproach for Christ's greater riches, than to have all the treasures of Egypt."[60]

Three months later, Preston Taylor cheerfully announced that W. H. Brown had returned to the Christian Church fold. He then appealed to his readers to "reach out our hand and add, in my Father's house

---

[58] Preston Taylor, "Our Colored Brethren," *Christian Standard* 15 (May 8, 188): 149.

[59] H. S. Berry, "Our Colored Brethren," *Christian Standard* 15 (June 12, 1880): 189.

[60] H. S. Berry, "Our Colored Brethren," *Christian Standard* 16 (August 20, 1881): 272.

there is bread enough and to spare." Brown, after acknowledging that he had joined the Methodists in June of 1881, felt guilt-ridden for

> making merchandise of the Gospel for the treasure of Methodism; of which sin I have repented a thousand times, though my circumstances in life drove me to this. But thank God, I have come home and confessed my sin before God and His Church, and I ask the forgiveness of the brotherhood at large.[61]

S. W. Womack, a Christian Church preacher in Fosterville, Tennessee, filled in at the Gay Street congregation for "the venerable" H. S. Berry. Upon arriving in Nashville, Womack was warmly received and "most kindly entertained." He then noted that the evening audience was much larger than the morning crowd. He reported,

> At night we were much encouraged, having a pressing and thronging crowd to speak to. Attention splendid. Miss Calhoun, the organist, faithfully did her part in making good music; and to make things short I must say this people surely have the work at heart, and such a church is a great power in that part of the land, and can not be too highly spoken of, for its work's sake; and I must say every visit I make to Nashville I am more encouraged by meeting so many good brethren and sisters, who bid me welcome any time under the roof of their houses.[62]

In the spring of 1882, H. S. Berry gave the dedicatory address for the black Christian Church in Paducah, Kentucky, whose building had burned down two years earlier. He specifically lauded D. R. Wilkins, a man of "iron will," who refused to "fold his hands and do nothing whimsically cry, 'Oh! we must yield to the inevitable; 'tis the work of Providence; don't complain; don't try to do anything else.'" After highlighting Wilkins's diligent labor for the past seven years, Berry asserted, "We preached in the old house in June 1880, and in the new one in 1882, and can say, like the prophet, the glory of this latter house is greater than that of the former." He then prayed that

---

[61] W. H. Brown, "Our Colored Brethren," *Christian Standard* 16 (November 19, 1881): 373.

[62] S. W. Womack, "Our Colored Brethren," *Christian Standard* 17 (April 18, 1882): 107.

a "few more D. R. Wilkinses may providentially spring up to do noble deeds in the cause of the Saviour."[63]

In the spring of 1880, H. S. Berry became embroiled in controversy when he responded negatively to three questions raised in Preston Taylor's column about Samuel Lowery, Peter Lowery, and Daniel Wadkins. To the first inquiry, "Is Samuel Lowery, a representative for the Silk Worm Manual Labor Institute, a preacher of the Christian Church and in fellowship with the Gay Street Christian Church?" Berry answered: "No!" To the second question, "Is Peter Lowery a preacher for the Gay Street congregation in 'good standing'?" Berry again replied: No! To the third inquiry, "Is Elder Daniel Wadkins a member of your congregation?" Berry asserted: "No! He is our most formidable enemy. He is not a member with this congregation and never was, and we are not anxious that he ever shall be." He further called Wadkins an "evil genius, so bad has been his deportment that not a congregation of color holds him in any regard scarcely at all. As for us, he dare not enter our pulpit."[64]

Samuel Lowery, a gospel preacher in Ohio before returning to Tennessee, called Berry's accusations a "wicked, malicious, villainous lie, and he has prostituted the dignified office of Christian teacher."[65] Wadkins was even more harsh in his response to Berry's allegations, explaining that he was baptized into the "Christian congregation that existed in Nashville" before the Civil War. When the decision was made to establish a separate Christian Church for African Americans, Wadkins chose to remain with the white congregation. "I have lived in this city ever since," confessed Wadkins, "and I have never learned that my decision was wrong. This being thirty years ago, it was before my slanderer was born into the world."[66]

Furthermore, Wadkins vigorously opposed the practices of Berry and the Gay Street Christian Church, who hosted

> fairs, festivals, and other entertainments in the house used ostensibly for Christian worship, and giving out twenty-five

---

[63] H. S. Berry, "Our Colored Brethren" *Christian Standard* 17 (June 24, 1882): 195.

[64] H. S. Berry, "Our Colored Brethren," *Christian Standard* 17 (May 29, 1880): 173.

[65] Samuel Lowery, "Our Colored Brethren," *Christian Standard* 17 (June 19, 1880): 197.

[66] Daniel Wadkins, "Our Colored Brethren," *Christian Standard* 17 (July 3, 1880): 213.

dollar prizes to the young female that would sell the most tickets or bring in the most money, as H. S. Berry and some others did, gallery, to please and entertain the world, the flesh, and the devil.

Wadkins further disapproved of Berry traveling to Chattanooga and Little Rock to "secret society meetings," namely, Masonic lodges. Wadkins said he had advised Berry against this "worldly and fleshly course" of aligning with and obligating himself to "secret societies" in Nashville. Wadkins then concluded, "I became his enemy when I told him the truth."[67]

The foregoing exchange shows that extra-congregational practices created tension among African Americans in the Stone-Campbell movement. The dispute between Berry and Wadkins foreshadowed the rupture that would be formalized in the late nineteenth and early twentieth centuries. In 1889, white church leaders of the Sand Creek Church of Christ in Sand Creek, Illinois, issued an "Address and Declaration" to reject those who taught and practiced things not "found in the New Testament," such "innovations" as fairs, festivals, "man-made society for missionary work," and the like.[68]

Notwithstanding the impending division, Preston Taylor experienced firsthand the spiritual and emotional fracture that white and black Disciples went through. Moreover, the religious development of Taylor lends credence to the thesis of scholar David Edwin Harrell that as Disciples grew in the big cities, they adopted and adapted to the culture of the urban cities in the North, openly using church choirs, hired pastors, instruments of music in worship, missionary societies, and the like.[69] Taylor's material prosperity in some way shaped his practices of open fellowship, worshiping with mechanical instruments, and wearing lofty titles such as reverend, elder, and pastor. Still, even though he acquired affluence during his Nashville years, he used his influence to aid the poor and outcasts in his local community and beyond.

---

[67] Ibid.

[68] Leroy Garrett, *The Stone-Campbell Movement: The Story of the American Restoration Movement* (Joplin, MO: College Press, 1981/2006), 381, 392.

[69] Harrell, *Sources of Division*, 84.

In essence, Taylor's experiences as a church leader in postbellum Kentucky proved a mixed bag of failures and successes, pains and gains. The collapse of the New Castle Bible School, two failed marriages, the death of an infant child, and the passing of his dear mother doubtlessly dampened his spirit; yet his success as a church builder, a practical theologian, a religious paper editor, and a local preacher—"his highest calling"—catapulted him to national prominence. Indeed, by the time the New Castle Bible School collapsed, Taylor had relocated 250 miles away to Nashville, Tennessee, in search of a new start in a new city. He arrived in the Athens of the South with pains and gains and with the same dogged determination to make life better for his fellow African Americans. Even though his New Castle Bible School project fell through, he learned invaluable lessons about fundraising and networking. Disappointed but never daunted, Preston Taylor rolled up his sleeves and licked his wounds, determined to "pave the way for his people."

Four

Holding on to Jesus

African American Women in Disciples of Christ

A virtuous woman is a crown to her husband: but she that maketh ashamed is as rottenness in his bones.
—Proverbs 12:4

Now there was at Joppa a certain disciple named Tabitha, which by interpretation is called Dorcas: this woman was full of good works and almsdeeds which she did.
—Acts 9:36

In the spring of 1879, Pastor Preston Taylor attended an all-women meeting at the High Street Christian Church in Mt. Sterling, Kentucky. According to their preacher, a "'large number' of High Street sisters meet weekly, pay five cents each, take contracts for quilting and sewing, and have been a 'great help' to the church. They have their own President, Secretary, Treasurer, etc., and it is astonishing to see how nicely they conduct their business."

Buoyed by what he witnessed in the sisters' meeting, Taylor urged his listeners to support the work of Christian women. "All of our churches ought by all means," wrote the evangelist, "to encourage the woman's work in this way, by giving them the meeting to themselves for consultation, and they will always find some way of assistance for the church."

Allowing industrious women to operate independently, he continued, "will infuse life into the working element of the church, and we will soon see an organized band of women in all the Churches of Christ."¹

One of the young ladies attending the sisters' meeting at the High Street congregation was Anna Hoffman. Recognizing her beauty and talent, Taylor recommended that she and Mollie Meeks prepare to read essays at the next annual Disciples Missionary Convention, scheduled for the following year in Winchester, Kentucky.² Before the next convention, however, the preacher had divorced his wife, Ella (or Ellen), fallen in love with Anna, and married her on June 11, 1880.³

Some weeks after her marriage to Taylor, Anna presented an essay entitled, "Redeeming the Time," based on Ephesians 5:16. The speech urged her listeners

> to redeem the time, to gather up its fragments, to secure its *remnants*, to see to it that no hours or moments shall escape us unimproved. Let us have done with idle dreaming, waiting and fancying, and let us strive every day to complete something which shall tell for the good of our Sunday schools and fast ripen into Christianity.⁴

Mrs. Taylor's presentation reveals a young lady with biblical knowledge, in addition to being a talented writer and an inspiring moral instructor. Furthermore, like her husband, Anna Taylor appeared to be a woman of action, a woman of God who believed in making the most of her time.

Six months into their marriage, however, tragedy struck the Taylor household, when Preston Taylor's mother, Betty, passed away "with the disease of dropsy."⁵ Readers of the "Our Colored Brethren" column expressed "great sympathy" over her transition, and many regretted not being able to attend her funeral because of inclement weather.⁶ Sorrow again invaded the Taylor family when

---

¹ Preston Taylor, "Our Colored Brethren," *Christian Standard* 14 (May 3, 1879): 141.

² Preston Taylor, "Our Colored Brethren," *Christian Standard* (June 14, 1879): 189.

³ "Marriage Certificate" (June 1880) in the Preston Taylor File at the Disciples of Christ Historical Society (DCHS) at Bethany, West Virginia.

⁴ Annie Taylor, "Our Colored Brethren," *Christian Standard* 15 (July 24, 1880): 237.

⁵ Preston Taylor, "Our Colored Brethren," *Christian Standard* 17 (January 21, 1882): 19.

⁶ A. Merchant, "Our Colored Brethren," *Christian Standard* 17 (January 28, 1882): 27. J. C. Graves, "Our Colored Brethren," *Christian Standard* 17 (March 18, 1882): 75.

Errett Mitchell, the one-month-old son of Preston and Anna, passed away. The following summer, the couple announced the birth of a little girl, Hattie Whitney.[7] There is no known extant evidence that this baby survived to adulthood.

Notwithstanding the lack of information regarding details of family, it is clear that at some point, the marriage of Preston and Anna Taylor unraveled. Did the preacher commit marital infidelity? Did the preacher overextend himself by immersing himself in too many business and educational enterprises? Perhaps his experience as a Union soldier exposed him to a culture of unfaithfulness. Scholar Tera Hunter has noted:

> The atmosphere of the Civil War also encouraged bigamy, as the insecurity of life and the adventure of military service gave men more options for entering and exiting relationships with impunity beyond their home turfs, where their marital status would have been known. In many cases they hid their existing relationships, but in many others they did not, perhaps assuming that the new circumstances would likely sever them from their former ties.[8]

Even though Taylor was just fifteen years old when he found himself in the throes of the Civil War and almost twenty when ushered out of the Union Army, we still do not know the exact causes of his annulments. Yet, what remains clear is that he perceptively understood how substantively and significantly women—including his mother, wife, and High Street sisters—contributed to the growth and development of African American Disciples. Therefore, he cast his full support and succor behind their efforts to serve the kingdom of God.

'If It Wasn't for the Women'

In the summer of 1879, Preston Taylor traveled forty-six miles from Mt. Sterling to Versailles, Kentucky, where he preached and strengthened twelve African American Disciples. Taylor's preaching yielded one conversion, as he readily discovered that the "opposition

---

[7] Preston Taylor, "Our Colored Brethren," *Christian Standard* 16 (July 2, 1881): 216. See also, Preston Taylor, "Our Colored Brethren," *Christian Standard* 16 (July 15, 1882): 219.

[8] Tera Hunter, *Bound in Wedlock: Slave and Free Black Marriage in the Nineteenth Century* (Cambridge, MA: Harvard University Press, 2017), 219.

to our people is very great, but the faith of the few disciples is fully able to stand." He singled out Sister Jane Waters, a black Stone-Campbell adherent who was married to a Baptist preacher. Taylor reported that the Baptist clergyman "publicly denounces her faith; says he loves her, but will not eat at the table of the Lord with her until she becomes a Baptist," adding, "his wife does not belong to any church, but to a Campbellite society." Mr. Waters even threatened to abandon his wife, "if she did not join his church." Sister Waters replied that she would gladly "hold on to Jesus and let him [her husband] go." The faith, resolve, and dedication of Sister Waters impressed and inspired Taylor to say of the fledgling congregation at Versailles: "We have some good material here, and it is a very important place for a church."[9]

Thirteen miles east of Versailles stood Lexington, Kentucky, where A. M. Ayers toiled for a Christian Church. Ayers lamented the passing of Sister James Fisher, a "consistent Christian woman, but she has gone to reap her reward." Ayers noted that Mrs. Fisher called her dear children to her bedside, bade them good by [sic], and be good children; called her husband; and said to him, "You do the best you can. I am going to my Father. Good by."[10] Sister Fisher fell asleep at her home on July 16, 1879.

In the early nineteenth century, a small number of women in the Stone-Campbell movement functioned as church planters, evangelists, and missionaries. Some church historians recognize Clara Hale Babcock as the first woman ordained for preaching in the Disciples of Christ tradition in 1889, but Sarah Lue Bostick, an African American woman, also emerged as an influential preacher and organizer in the late nineteenth century.[11] These few examples attest that women in the Stone-Campbell movement bore a heavy burden of sexism. Even though women in the Stone-Campbell movement worked in subordinate roles, their work was pivotal.

While Anglo women in the Stone-Campbell movement bore a heavy burden of sexism, African American women shouldered a

---

[9] Preston Taylor, "Our Colored Brethren," *Christian Standard* 14 (August 2, 1879): 245.

[10] Ibid.

[11] Debra B. Hull, "Women in Ministry," in Foster et al. (eds), *The Encyclopedia of the Stone-Campbell Movement*, 776-777. Harrell, *Sources of Division in the Disciples of Christ, 1865–1900*, 257. Harrell has observed: "In the 1870's women worked in a subordinate role in Disciples churches. Generally, women were banned from preaching, serving as elders or in a role of authority, and did not lead in any public service."

double burden of sexism and racism. Scholar Deborah Gray White has examined the "double oppression" black women experienced in the pre–Civil War era,[12] and historian Jacqueline Jones noted that African American women in the Postbellum period also carried a "doubly disadvantaged status" of racism and sexism.[13] Notwithstanding these moral burdens and social barriers, African American women helped make the black church, in the words of scholar Evelyn Brooks Higginbotham, the "most powerful institution of racial self-help in the African American community."[14] As this chapter will show, the female black cohorts of Preston Taylor strengthened and solidified fledgling congregations across the Mid-South and beyond, and helped pave the way for stronger churches generations ahead. Thus, in response to scholar Cheryl Townsend Gilkes's thesis, *If It Wasn't for the Women*,[15] Taylor would utter a hearty, "Amen."

---

[12] Deborah Gray White, *Ar'nt I a Woman? Female Slaves in the Plantation South* (New York: W. W. Norton, 1985), 23.

[13] Jacqueline Jones, *Labor of Love, Labor of Sorrow: Black Women, Work, and the Family, from Slavery to the Present* (New York: Vintage Books, 1986), 3. Edward J. Robinson, *I Was under a Heavy Burden: The Life of Annie C. Tuggle* (Abilene, TX: Abilene Christian University Press, 2011). Robinson has argued that Annie C. Tuggle (1890–1976) and other African American women in Churches of Christ bore a complexity of triple burdens of sexism, racism, and religion, as their rigid theological perspectives ostracized them from their black religious neighbors.

[14] Evelyn Brooks Higginbotham, *Righteous Discontent: The Women's Movement in the Black Baptist Church, 1880–1920* (Cambridge, MA: Harvard University Press, 1981), 1. Historian Paul Harvey, *Freedom's Coming: Religious Culture and the Shaping of the South from the Civil War through the Civil Rights Era* (Chapel Hill, NC: University of North Carolina Press, 2005), 70. Harvey has observed, "Black women in the Jim Crow era vigorously pursued the work of evangelization and moral uplift, raising significant sums for benevolent endeavors and filling more pews in church than men." Bettye Collier-Thomas, *Jesus, Jobs, and Justice: African American Women and Religion* (New York: Alfred A. Knopf, 2010), xxx. In her exhaustive and perceptive study, Collier-Thomas agreed with Higginbotham, noting that the "African American church as an institution would not exist without the membership and financial support of black women."

[15] Cheryl Townsend Gilkes, *If It Wasn't for the Women: Black Women's Experience and Womanist Culture in Church and Community* (Maryknoll, NY: Orbis Books, 2001). When probing the contributions of black women in the Church of God in Christ, scholar Anthea D. Butler has observed that assertive women in COGIC served as counselors to pastors, leaders of youth, and "spiritual avatars to the congregation." Anthea D. Butler, *Women in the Church of God in Christ: Making a Sanctified World* (Chapel Hill, NC: University of North Carolina Press, 2007), 12.

Women of Distinction

Preston Taylor's "Our Colored Brethren" column reveals that black women in Disciples of Christ contributed significantly to the growth and development of their chosen fellowship in the late nineteenth century. They wrote poetry, delivered speeches, taught classes, raised funds, and supported their pastors by lavishing them with generous gifts. The polity and theology of Taylor was inclusive in that it made ample room for the presence and participation of African American women in the Disciples of Christ.

Susie King

Susie King was a devout member of the Christian Church in Lexington, Kentucky. In the spring of 1879, she published a poem entitled, "Love," in which she urged her audience to "learn to live indeed." The middle stanza of the poem went like this:

> Christ has said, "Love each other";
> Thus the world my people know.
> He that loveth not his brother
> Is a child of wrath and woe.
> Christians, let us think on this—
> Let us prove that we are His.[16]

This verse demonstrates a working knowledge of scripture, especially the gospel of John (13:34-35) and the Epistle of 1 John (3:18; 4:7).

Four years later, King composed an article, "The Value of Time and Knowledge," and stressed that time was the "most precious thing in all the world." Knowing that some of her readers were prone to idleness, she urged, "Only take care to gather up the fragments of time, and you will never want leisure for the reading of useful books." In King's estimation, devouring wholesome books helped to mold one's character. "A taste for useful reading is an effectual preservative from vice," she wrote, adding, "Next to the fear of God implanted in the heart, nothing is a better safeguard to character than the love of good works."[17]

---

[16] Susie M. King, "Our Colored Brethren," *Christian Standard* 14 (April 5, 1879): 109.

[17] Susie M. King, "Our Colored Brethren," *Christian Standard* 18 (February 17, 1883): 77.

A proper use of time would lead to an increase of knowledge. King asked, "What is it that mainly distinguishes man from a brute? Knowledge. What makes the vast difference there is between savage and civilized nations? Knowledge. What forms the principal difference between men as they appear in the same society? Knowledge. Knowledge is power."[18] For a people who had been denied the opportunity for literacy, King challenged her audience to empower themselves by using their time properly.

Annie Fraizier

In the summer of 1881, Annie Fraizier read a poem on the mode of baptism at the Danville Christian Sunday School Convention in Danville, Kentucky. She directed her poem at religious groups who downplayed the significance of baptism and against those who practiced sprinkling and pouring as the proper mode of baptism. The poem, in part, went like this:

> Although I write it now in verse,
> That to baptize is to immerse;
> I say, to me this does appear,
> And I will try to make it clear:
>
> John to baptize by heaven was sent,
> And to the river Jordan went;
> And in the river, we're apprised,
> The people were by him baptized. ...
>
> Buried by baptism, interred.
> That is the meaning of the Word.
> Such is the language of our version,
> And looks a great deal like immersion.[19]

African American leaders in the Disciples of Christ applauded Fraizer's creativity and without doubt appropriated her poem when discussing the subject of baptism with their religious neighbors. Her poem then succinctly captured and reinforced what black Disciples believed about salvation.

---

[18] Ibid.
[19] Annie Fraizer, "Our Colored Brethren," *Christian Standard* 16 (August 6, 1881): 253.

Lizzie Carter

Lizzie Carter, a young Disciple in Louisville, Kentucky, used the *Christian Standard* column to tout the "missionary worker" in her article, "A Lord's Day School Missionary Worker." According to Carter, the missionary worker, with his "kind words and instructions," can turn wayward persons from the "path of vice, to the path of virtue, and they be made to rejoice." She rejected the erroneous notion that the designation "missionary belongs to males only," explaining: "The young, the old, the grave, the gay, including all Christians at large, and the mother at home, might be missionary workers."[20]

Carter also lamented the juvenile delinquency she saw in her community. She witnessed daily the "wagon and train carrying prisoners to the penitentiaries, jails, and work houses. Some are but ten, twelve and fifteen years old." Carter then asked, "Why have they chosen the path of vice so young? I answer, because some of them have never had the guiding hand of a missionary mother to lead them to higher principles." In her mind, the "Lord's day school is the nursery of the church, and from it grows many a true and brave Christian heart." Thus, she concluded, "Then let us all go to work, be missionary workers, and I believe that God will bless us."[21]

Four years after composing the piece about missionary workers, Lizzie Carter married Henry Clarke at the High Street Church in Mt. Sterling, Kentucky. Preston Taylor officiated the union.[22]

Clara Schell

Clara Schell, a black devotee of the Stone-Campbell movement, surfaced in Taylor's "Our Colored Brethren" column in the fall of 1881. Stationed in Washington, D.C., "the negro's heaven," Schell saw firsthand the deplorable conditions of African Americans in their nation's capital. She winced seeing impoverished black people living in a "small, illy-vented and poorly constructed houses." Even though many black residents were "like cattle in pens," Schell viewed them as "human beings with souls to save."[23] In the *Christian Standard*,

---

[20] Lizzie Carter, "Our Colored Brethren," *Christian Standard* 14 (June 21, 1879): 197.

[21] Ibid.

[22] Preston Taylor, "Our Colored Brethren," *Christian Standard* 18 (November 24, 1883): 445.

[23] Clara Schell, "A Sketch of the Colored People of Washington, D.C.—1," *Christian Monitor* XXI (August 1882): 369. Many thanks for Shelly Jacobs for sharing this source with me. See also Harrell, *Sources of Division*, 193.

she divulged her action plan to assist black citizens in the District of Columbia. Taylor cast his full support behind Schell's mission work and used his column to rally black Christians, stating in bold print: "LET US SECOND THE MOTION."[24]

Schell explained to *Christian Standard* readers,

> My plan of work is this: Secure a place at once to start a mission Lord's day school in, and once, or more, during the week have preaching by my husband W. H. Schell, and Bro. F. D. Power; in this way work up an interest and make converts to the primitive gospel.[25]

Her appeal stirred the pocket books of black Disciples. H. M. Ayers, pastor of a Christian Church in Lexington, Kentucky, vowed to "do all in my power" to plant a black Disciples congregation in Washington, D.C. Injecting humor into his plea, Ayers commented, "No better time to work, said a blacksmith, than when the iron is hot, and we call upon the preachers and leading brethren of the various States to set the time when the collection shall be made."[26]

Martha Smith, an African American Christian in Cincinnati, Ohio, had recently returned from Washington, D.C., and found there just one black Disciple. Thus, she urged, "all we need there is *ten workers* like Sister Schell. I can but trust her hands will be held up by the brotherhood generally."[27]

J. C. Graves, a spiritual leader of a Christian Church in Paris, Kentucky, approved the work in the nation's capital and praised "God for raising Sister Schell up to be a light to the people at the Capital of this great nation of ours."

Mrs. Schell's mission school opened on April 9, 1882, with twenty-seven children and twelve instructors.[28]

Taylor, as editor of the "Our Colored Brethren" column, prodded his readership to support Schell's effort, and he added, "It should

---

[24] Preston Taylor, "Our Colored Brethren," *Christian Standard* 16 (November 19, 1881): 373.

[25] Clara Schell, "Our Colored Brethren," *Christian Standard* 16 (November 26, 1881): 381.

[26] H. M. Ayers, "Our Colored Brethren," *Christian Standard* 16 (December 24, 1881): 413.

[27] Martha Smith, "Our Colored Brethren," *Christian Standard* 16 (December 24, 1881): 413.

[28] J. C. Graves, "Our Colored Brethren," *Christian Standard* 17 (March 11, 1882): 75.

be a pride to our churches to assist in this much needed cause. The white brethren have given, but they have much to be done, and we must rally to this call."[29]

Two weeks after the mission opened, Schell reported eighty-two scholars. Taylor noted,

> That is far better than a great many old schools can record for one day's work, and it ought to inspire the hearts of Mrs. Clara Schell and her true helpmates in the work at Washington, and we can not urge too strongly upon those who have the means to give, to help in this work.[30]

The following month, Schell announced that the women at the High Street Christian Church in Mt. Sterling, Kentucky, had raised $25 to "pay for half the time for an evangelist."[31] The women of Taylor's flock understood the essential nature of gospel preaching; thus, while they were interested in developing the mind, they were more concerned with converting the soul. The High Street sisters had come to see that, just as their own preacher's "highest calling" was to proclaim the word, it was their aim also to support the propagation of the "primitive Gospel."

'Good Sisters Will Take Care of Their Preacher'

In the winter of 1881, Samuel Buckner, the pastor of a Disciples Church in Paris, Kentucky, preached in Germantown and yielded four conversions; one of them was an "old lady aged 80 years. Baptized in a bath tub."[32] Perhaps to reward their hard-working preacher, the church bought Buckner a "new suit of clothes." The generous ladies reported, "We should now like to see Bro. Samuel Buckner stepping around in them. He is worthy of the gift. Suit again."[33]

This excerpt attests that Buckner, like many black Disciple preachers, filled the pulpit at multiple congregations. Moreover,

---

[29] Taylor, "Our Colored Brethren," *Christian Standard* 17 (April 22, 1882): 123. See also Clara Schell, "A Sketch of the Colored People of Washington, D. C.—2," *Christian Monitor* XXI (October 1882): 472. Harrell, *Sources of Division*, 193.

[30] Preston Taylor, "Our Colored Brethren," *Christian Standard* 17 (April 29, 1882): 133.

[31] Clara Schell, "Washington Mission," *Christian Monitor* XXI (May 1882): 224.

[32] Samuel Buckner, "Our Colored Brethren," *Christian Standard* 16 (March 12, 1881): 93.

[33] Samuel Buckner, "Our Colored Brethren," *Christian Standard* 16 (August 6, 1881): 253.

it shows that African American Christians in general and African American women in particular highly regarded their preachers. Writing in the early twentieth century, W. E. B. Du Bois highlighted the significance of black preachers in their communities, declaring, "The Preacher is the most unique personality developed by the Negro on American soil. A leader, a politician, an orator, a 'boss,' an intriguer, an idealist,—all these he is, and ever, too, the centre of a group of men, now twenty, now a thousand in number."[34]

Civil rights activist James Farmer went further than Du Bois and asserted,

> The black preacher, especially in the South, is king in a private kingdom. Whether learned or ignorant, he is both oracle and soothsayer, showman and pontiff, father image to all and husband-by-proxy to the unattached women in the church and others whose mates are either inadequate or missing. More than a priest, he is less only than God.[35]

H. M. Ayers, an African American minister in Lexington, Kentucky, confirmed the veracity of the foregoing observations. During the Christmas season of 1882, women of the black Disciples congregation in Lexington showered Ayers and his wife with many material and monetary gifts. He bragged,

> You have no idea how many good things were brought to my house on Christmas night by the good sisters. Well, you know the good sisters will take care of their preacher, and I tell you it was a grand success. Meat, chicken, coffee, sugar cakes, pickles, and, indeed, everything that is good for a preacher and his wife was brought in. I will tell you something more: they brought me some dollars, yea, silver dollars. I think we have the best church in the State, or indeed, any State, and I thank God we live in peace, and have done so for twelve years.[36]

---

[34] W. E. B. Du Bois, *The Souls of Black Folk* (New York: Penguin, 1903/2012), 162.

[35] James Farmer, *Lay Bare the Heart: An Autobiography of the Civil Rights Movement* (Fort Worth, TX: Texas Christian University Press, 1985), 33.

[36] H. M. Myers, "Our Colored Brethren," *Christian Standard* 18 (January 27, 1883): 48.

Not to be outdone by the women in Germantown and Lexington, the sisters in Preston Taylor's congregation blessed their leader with a new wardrobe. "The ladies of the Mt. Sterling church," reported the *Christian Standard*, "clothed the editor of this column with a new garb, that feels as comfortable as it looks these cool hours." Indeed, twenty-four years later, when Taylor had become the pastor for the Lea Avenue Christian Church in Nashville, Tennessee, members there showered him with a "handsome suit of clothes, hat and gloves before leaving" for traveling out of state.[37] Taking their cue perhaps from their black Baptist, Methodist, and other religious neighbors, there appears to have been a developing culture among African American Disciples of Christ that required that preachers take care of their members and that members, especially the sisters, take care of their preachers.

Living and Dying in the 'Triumph of Faith'

The "Our Colored Brethren" column contains many references to African American Disciples who lived and died in the faith. These eulogistic snippets not only offer a glimpse into their Christian character but also furnish a view into the broader fellowship of black Disciples of Christ. Fanny Batterson, who passed away in the fall of 1879, had been a Christian for thirty-seven years. Preston Taylor called her a "good wife, a Christian lady and a good neighbor, having lived a practical example of piety to all who knew her."[38]

In a community four miles west of Mt. Sterling, Taylor met an eighty-seven-year-old woman who joined the Christian Church from its inception in the county. He called Nancy Williams a "model of Christianity."[39] In the spring of 1880, the he eulogized Sister Caroline King, a "devoted Christian" and a mother of twenty-four children— "four of them remain to weep their loss. Twenty of them are with her in the better land." Her last words were, "He that believeth and is baptized shall be saved."[40]

---

[37] Preston Taylor, "Our Colored Brethren," *Christian Standard* 18 (October 27, 1883): 413. See also, "A Presentation," *Nashville Globe* (January 18, 1907): 4.

[38] Preston Taylor, "Our Colored Brethren," *Christian Standard* 14 (September 13, 1879): 293.

[39] Preston Taylor, "Our Colored Brethren," *Christian Standard* 15 (January 31, 1880): 109.

[40] Preston Taylor, "Our Colored Brethren," *Christian Standard* 15 (April 3, 1880): 109.

Maggie Price came under Taylor's influence when he preached in Cincinnati, Ohio, in the spring of 1879, but she passed away the following fall. The "Our Colored Brethren" editor recorded, "She was between sixteen and seventeen years of age, but in faith she seemed to be an old warrior."[41] Taylor similarly mourned the lost of Ann Coleman, a Disciple for twenty-five years, whom he called an "earnest Christian."[42] The High Street Christian Church at Mt. Sterling bade farewell to another faithful woman, Sister Mary Banks, a "devout Christian until called to her reward." The eulogist used Luke 10:42 as his funeral text: "Mary hath chosen that good part which shall not be taken away from her."[43]

After the departure of another "devoted Christian," Sister Bettie Johnson, from the Mt. Sterling flock, Taylor lamented: "This makes 7 who we lost out of this congregation this year; but we are thankful to report that all are now well."[44] After Mary Craig fell asleep in Paris, Kentucky, it was noted, "She was a bright Christian soldier in the army of the Lord."[45] Louisa Wickliffe, a member of the Christian Church for a decade, suffered a long time from consumption, but she "died in the triumph of faith."[46]

J. C. Graves, pastor of a Christian Church in Paris, Kentucky, announced that 108-year-old Sister Mary Taylor "died in the faith, looking for the blessed hope."[47] Benjamin King, a preacher in Ohio, announced that sixty-eight-year-old Sister Phoebe Dixon "lived a devoted Christian life, and died as she had lived."[48] King also eulogized Sister Martha Sanders, whom he called,

---

[41] Preston Taylor, "Our Colored Brethren," *Christian Standard* 15 (October 9, 1880): 325.

[42] Preston Taylor, "Our Colored Brethren," *Christian Standard* 16 (May 21, 1881): 165.

[43] Preston Taylor, "Our Colored Brethren," *Christian Standard* 17 (May 13, 1882): 147.

[44] Preston Taylor, "Our Colored Brethren," *Christian Standard* 16 (June 11, 1881): 189.

[45] Preston Taylor, "Our Colored Brethren," *Christian Standard* 17 (June 3, 1882): 171.

[46] R. E. Hathaway, "Our Colored Brethren," *Christian Standard* 17 (July 8, 1882): 213.

[47] J. C. Graves, "Our Colored Brethren," *Christian Standard* 18 (January 18, 1883): 17.

[48] Benjamin King, "Our Colored Brethren," *Christian Standard* 18 (March 3, 1883): 101.

[a] woman of upright principles and faithful to every trust placed in her. She was also noted for her industrious habits, and many a time after a laborious task of doing a day's washing when her body was weary and needed rest, she would sit up all night with the sick and soothe the sufferer with her kind, gentle ways, which are grateful to the sick and afflicted.[49]

In the summer of 1883, Taylor reported the "sad news" that the house of Sister Alexander Campbell in Lexington, Kentucky, and the house of Sister Ellen Carter in Knoxville, Tennessee, had burned to the ground. "These are widows indeed," lamented the editor, "who have been companions of devoted Christian men, and some assistance would be wise."[50]

Twenty-year-old Florence Henderson, an African American Christian in Concord, Tennessee, exclaimed before her passing, "Oh, I am so happy in the Lord." She then requested that her parents, sisters, and classmates meet her in heaven, stating, "I am ready to be offered up into the hands of my beloved Lord."[51]

C. H. Lee, a leader in Normal, Illinois, informed *Christian Standard* readers of fourteen-year-old Clara McFadden, who died of the disease of consumption. Lee reported,

> Clara was perfectly composed during her sickness until the last hours of her life, when she began to be weary of life and its labors. She said she desired to be on that beautiful shore she had so often heard her mother speak of, where sickness, sorrow, pain and death are felt and feared no more.[52]

The funeral announcements and eulogistic remarks about black women in the Christian Church, presented in Taylor's "Our Colored Brethren" section, reveal the significant contributions of African American women in the Disciples of Christ. Certain women stood out. Clara Schell toiled to provide moral and spiritual uplift for black

---

[49] Benjamin King, "Our Colored Brethren," *Christian Standard* 18 (March 31, 1883): 148.

[50] Preston Taylor, "Our Colored Brethren," *Christian Standard* 18 (July 14, 1883): 293.

[51] Preston Taylor, "Our Colored Brethren" *Christian Standard* 18 (October 13, 1883): 397.

[52] C. H. Lee, "Our Colored Brethren" *Christian Standard* 19 (June 21, 1884): 197.

residents in the nation's capital. Susie King and Anna Taylor lifted their poetic voices to offer ethical guidance and instruction to black men and women in the Stone-Campbell movement.

The women referenced in this chapter emerged from the dark shadows of chattel enslavement and labored in the dusk of *de jure* segregation to shine a light of hope and to bless their people, black people, morally and spiritually. More significantly, all of the women in this chapter were connected to Preston Taylor in some way, as their letters, reports, and stories came through his hands in the mail; and he subsequently presented their tales to the readership of the *Christian Standard*. In short, Taylor applauded the black women in the Stone-Campbell movement, because he knew fully that African American sisters blessed tremendously the fellowship of African American Disciples.

Part 3

Trials and Triumphs in Tennessee, 1885-1916

Five

'Fighting the Devil in Nashville'

The Complex Worlds of African Americans in Middle Tennessee

Put on the whole armour of God, that ye may be able to stand against the wiles of the devil.
—Ephesians 6:11

Be sober, be vigilant; because your adversary the devil, as a roaring lion, walketh about, seeking whom he may devour.
—1 Peter 5:8

In January of 1907, several African American denominations in Nashville, Tennessee, joined hands in a series of revival meetings to "wage a successful conflict against Satan and his host." Various black religious groups—including Presbyterians, Baptists, Methodists, and Preston Taylor's Lea Avenue Christian Church—participated in these praying and preaching services. The basic aim of these revivals was to "do something in the name of the suffering Savior." Black Christians in Nashville believed that earnest prayer and evangelistic preaching proved crucial to defeating the demonic forces vexing the African American community. The *Nashville Globe* dubbed the spiritual activity, "Fighting the Devil in Nashville."[1]

Taylor, of course, contributed to the ecumenical revivals, but he was more than a prayer warrior and an articulate pastor. He was,

---
[1] "Fighting the Devil in Nashville," *Nashville Globe* (April 12, 1907): 2.

according to one author, a "doer of the word."[2] Thus, he worked diligently beyond the pulpit and pew to uplift his people. In 1905, when white officials in Nashville legalized segregated streetcars, Taylor helped organize the Union Transportation Company (UTC) to launch a boycott against the new law. Black leaders called the Jim Crow statute an "eternal disgrace," designed to "humiliate, degrade, and stigmatize the Negro." According to historians August Meier and Elliott Rudwick, the transportation company was formed to protest discrimination, to rally black businesses for racial solidarity, and to resolve practical transportation problems faced by black participants of the boycott.[3]

The boycott began with enthusiasm, as the UTC's fundraisers yielded $16,000, with women raising most of it. The company's leaders purchased nine steam cars from the Mobile Machine Company of Tarrytown, New York. By 1907, however, the boycotters' passion had waned because the steam cars lacked power to climb Nashville's hills and because most black Nashvillians depended heavily on their white employers and feared retaliation.[4]

As the newly formed organization shut down, Taylor informed stockholders in a final meeting that a St. Louis Firm bought eight of the UTC's "electric automobiles," leaving a debt of $734.26 out of the original $20,000. He further explained that "he had in the beginning of the organization vowed himself heart and soul into the cause. He felt that what he had belonged to his people, if they would appreciate it." The *Nashville Globe* noted that Taylor provided an overview of the transportation company since its inception. The company's leader then lamented that they "never had sufficient funds."[5]

Taylor was a man of passion and zeal, a man who practiced integrity and transparency by providing stockholders (mostly women) detailed financial records. Self-sacrificing and selfless in his disposition, he did all he could for "his people." Additionally, he was a fighter of racial discrimination and social indignities. Launching the UTC was his way of "fighting the devil in Nashville."

---

[2] James L. Blair, "Preston Taylor: A Doer of the Word," in *The Untold Story: A Short History of Black Disciples*, ed. William K. Fox (St. Louis, MO: Christian Board of Publication, 1976), 32.

[3] Cited in August Meier and Elliott Rudwick, "Negro Boycotts of Jim Crow Streetcars in Tennessee," *American Quarterly* (Winter 1969): 760. See also, Faye Wellborn Robbins, "A World-within-a-World: Black Nashville, 1880-1915" (PhD diss. University of Arkansas, 1980), 214–215.

[4] Bobby L. Lovett, *The African-American History of Nashville, Tennessee, 1780–1930* (Fayetteville, AR: The University of Arkansas Press, 1999), 248–249.

[5] "Union Transportation Co.," *Nashville Globe* (May 3, 1907): 1.

'Let Us Have Peace'

Taylor, however, did not fight demonic influences in Nashville alone. Fellow black preachers crossed denominational lines and collaborated with him to help stem the rising tide of anti-black sentiment. Black newspapers, in conjunction with African American religious leaders, played a vital role in fighting the enemy in Middle Tennessee.

In 1905, Thomas Dixon Jr., a white Baptist preacher-turned-novelist, published *The Clansman*, a novel that portrayed black men as depraved beasts who roamed Southern communities assaulting white women. Dixon's book, set in the era of Reconstruction, interpreted the period as a horrible time for the white South subjected to "Negro rule"; these supposed grim conditions inspired the rise of the Ku Klux Klan, who assumed responsibility for protecting the virtue of white womanhood.

Dixon's novel became the basis for the 1915 blockbuster movie, *Birth of a Nation*. As scholars John Hope Franklin and Evelyn Brooks Higginbotham pointed out,

> *Birth of a Nation* told a most sordid and distorted story of Reconstruction-era black emancipation, enfranchisement, and violation of white womanhood. Its glorification of the Ku Klux Klan condoned vigilante violence, and the film did more than any other single medium to nurture and promote the myth of black domination and debauchery during Reconstruction.

Woodrow Wilson, a former classmate of Dixon's at Johns Hopkins University and president of the United States, lauded the film as "history writ in lightning."[6] But the *Nashville Globe* denounced

---

[6] John Hope Franklin and Evelyn Brooks Higginbotham, *From Slavery to Freedom: A History of African Americans* (New York: McGraw-Hill, 1947/2011), 357. Historian David W. Blight has insightfully noted: "Dixon's vicious version of the idea that blacks had caused the Civil War by their very presence, and that Northern radicalism during Reconstruction failed to understand that freedom had ushered blacks as a race into barbarism, neatly framed the story of the rise of heroic vigilantism in the South. Reluctantly, Klansmen—white men—had to take the law into their own hands in order to save Southern white womanhood from the sexual brutality of black men." David W. Blight, *Race and Reunion: The Civil War in American Memory* (Cambridge, MA: Harvard University Press, 2001), 111. See also Ibram X. Kendi, *Stamped from the Beginning: The Definitive History of Racist Ideas in America* (New York: Hachette, 2016/2017), 305–307.

the novelist as a "mob instigator, Negro murderer, inflammatory race persecutor."[7]

When *The Clansman* came to Nashville as a stage play in the winter of 1907, the Globe Publishing Company sent a reporter to visit the episode. The *Nashville Globe* reporter—who described himself as a law-obeying, tax-paying, "peaceable, Christian citizen"— expressed anger at being denied admission to the "murderous inflammatory exhibition for reasons unknown to him." Therefore, the black journalist relied on excerpts and appraisals from local white newspapers to provide his own assessment of the exhibition for black readers. The *Nashville American* was grateful that black residents of Nashville were barred from the show. "Wisely, it is believed," the reporter wrote, "did the management exclude negroes from the playhouse, for so powerfully was the spirit of the reconstruction period revived that it is probable they would have been in imminent danger of being forcibly expelled, if, indeed, more dramatic measures had not been resorted to."[8]

The *Nashville Banner* intimated sympathy for the *Clansman's* portrayal of the subjugation of white Southerners and the "fanaticism" of Northern politicians (the so-called Radical Republicans). Yet the paper insisted, "The South should not linger in bitter and unprofitable memories. It should not, at least, have its feelings harrowed by a recall of those evil days with their worst features accentuated and intensified with all the calcium effects of a stage production." The paper advised black residents in Nashville not to protest the dramatization, as the "best way to nullify such an influence, however, is to leave it unnoticed as far as possible."[9]

The black-owned paper, however, proposed allowing *Uncle Tom's Cabin* to follow the *Clansman's* play. African Americans in Nashville, according to the *Nashville Globe*, pledged full financial support, if the former production came to town. "Uncle Tom's Cabin, as written by Mrs. Harriet Beecher Stowe, did more, possibly to emancipate the Negroes than any other agency." Even though the 1852 antislavery novel was "dear" to black Americans and was "held in sacred memory," the editor urged: "Let us have peace," explaining:

---

[7] "Review of the 'Clansman'," *Nashville Globe* (February 1, 1907): 1.
[8] Ibid.
[9] Ibid.

While the Negroes love this play, and would pay more to see it than any other drama that is put upon the stage, yet because they found that it was offensive to their white neighbors they have abandoned the agitation of having it, and they do not encourage the circulation of the book.

African Americans, the *Nashville Globe* concluded, "have thought it best to let the dead past lie buried."[10]

Dixon's novel in substance enflamed race relations across the United States by insinuating that the black man's chief desire was to practice "social equality," that is, to "mix with the whites," especially white women. The *Nashville Globe* and other media outlets branded *The Clansman*'s propaganda as "absolutely false." James C. Russell, a *Globe* contributor, refuted Dixon's contention that the "Negro reaches his climax of sainthood when he marries a white woman," adding that it is not "social equality that the Negro of to-day contends for. He sees nothing in it that could afford either beauty or strength; and he is concerned only about the tangible things of life."[11]

Like most other black newspapers, the *Nashville Globe* used its columns to denounce white racism in all forms in the city of Nashville and beyond. The journal excoriated white streetcar passengers who violated Jim Crow laws by not sitting in the "whites only" section. "The colored passengers always obey this law," the editor fumed, "but white passengers boarding street cars sit anywhere except where they belong."[12] After a "rascally white fellow" indecently exposed himself to several black adolescent girls in Nashville, the paper castigated the perpetrator:

> The old scamp felt perfectly safe from arrest for his villainous performance. ... For an old white scamp to resort to such scoundrelly [sic] tactics to try to inflame the minds of children would stagger belief, if it were not a fact. A parallel case of such moral depravity could not be found in all heathendom.[13]

Racial violence also accompanied sexual deviancy. Black Nashvillians cringed when W. D. Graves, a white stable boss, shot

---
[10] Ibid.
[11] Ibid.
[12] "Breaking the Jim Crow Law," *Nashville Globe* (February 1, 1907): 4.
[13] "Bad White Man," *Nashville Globe* (May 3, 1907): 1.

and killed black laborer William Malone. When the latter approached the former about his pay, Graves "handed [Malone] the contents of a forty-five, without any apparent cause and in actual cold blood." Witnesses said they had heard Graves vent that he "intended to kill some 'niggers' before long."[14]

African Americans in Nashville also expressed outrage over police brutality, when white patrol officer R. McGovern reportedly slapped and jerked a five-year-old girl, Ora Humphrey. When the girl "dared to strike back," the officer grabbed her and summoned the aid of a white grocer, M. J. Murphy, who held the child's other hand while McGovern "brought his club into play, and with all the strength he could command struck the poor helpless girl with a telling blow on the head. The little creature was seen to reel and cringe in agony."

The policeman, according to the *Nashville Globe*, "seemed to be determined to beat the girl to death. A great gash was laid open that bared the skull and the blood was gushing out as water from a spout." Two priests witnessed the violence and confessed to never having seen "anything so brutal." The child was arrested, booked at the police station, and charged with disorderly conduct and resisting arrest. But little Ora did not remain in jail for long, as "friends of humanity" converged on the police station and made bail for the "unfortunate girl."[15] Preston Taylor was one of those "friends."

Other black Nashville residents testified to having had unpleasant encounters with Officer McGovern. Lizzie Harlan told an interviewer that the white patrolman had arrested her and her husband on the "pretext the neighbors had complained," but the judge dismissed the case because of insufficient evidence. The black paper complained that Mr. McGovern was the same officer who shot a man in the back.[16]

The Doctrine of Optimism

The *Nashville Globe* also kept the black community abreast of national events that affected the images and conditions of African Americans. The Brownsville Race Riot of 1906, which occurred when President Theodore Roosevelt dishonorably discharged 167 black soldiers of the 25th Infantry Regiment, occupied the front page of

---

[14] "Another Cold Blooded Murder," *Nashville Globe* (January 24, 1908): 1.
[15] "Policeman Beats Helpless Girl," *Nashville Globe* (June 19, 1908): 8.
[16] Ibid.

the Nashville paper.[17] The weekly journal studied the reports of Ray Stannard Baker, a muckraking journalist who probed America's racial divide and highlighted the inequities in Northern and Southern towns. The editor of the *Nashville Globe* called Baker's writing "refreshing" and urged that his articles "be read by every man in the South." The black paper also used the white journalist's reports to chide the African American community. Baker labeled black grocery stores in Atlanta "filthy," and they did not "compare very favorably with those run by 'Dagoes.'" The *Nashville Globe* then noted: "The same criticism will apply with equal force to some of our groceries in this city. Clean up." A month after the *Globe's* censure, the city of Nashville launched "Clean-Up Day," instructing its residents to cut their grass, dump their trash, clean their attics, and pick up all loose paper from their premises. Preston Taylor took the message to the black community by distributing circulars and visiting lodges. African American servants "asked for the day off so they could clean their own premises and were granted this courtesy." Like Booker T. Washington, Taylor's actions specifically rejected the notion that "civilization and hygiene were uniquely the provenance of whites."[18]

Racial oppression and physical violence against African Americans in other cities surfaced on the pages of the *Nashville Globe*. After the lynching of James Garden, a black man in Henrietta, Oklahoma, local white authorities gave black residents a forty-eight-hour notice to "get out of town."[19] Eight months later, the *Nashville Globe* informed its readership of a mass race riot in Springfield,

[17] "Mingo Saunders: Dismissed Sergeant on the Brownsville Raid," *Nashville Globe* (February 15, 1907): 1.

[18] "Following the Color Line," *Nashville Globe* (May 3, 1907): 4. In 1908, Ray Stannard Baker (1870–1946) published his findings in a noteworthy book titled, *Following the Color Line: An Account of Negro Citizenship in the American Democracy* (New York: Doubleday, 1908). "Cleaning Day, Big Success," *Nashville Banner* (June 6, 1907): 3. See also, Charlotte A. Williams, *The Centennial Club of Nashville: A History from 1905–77* (Nashville, TN: Centennial Club, 1978), 50. Carl A. Zimring, *Clean and White: A History of Environmental Racism in the United States* (New York: New York University Press, 2015), 102. Zimring points out: "The Nashville Institute for Negro Christian Workers trained young African American men and women as reformers in the mode of the settlement houses movement, with hopes that in a segregated society these reformers would uplift African Americans living in filthy, poor conditions." Even if Preston Taylor was not a member of this organization, he was aware of it and most likely supported its principles.

[19] "Negroes Ordered Away," *Nashville Globe* (December 27, 1907): 2, 6.

Illinois, which resulted in the deaths of nine black people, seven white residents (five of whom were killed by black residents), and the destruction of dozens of black homes and businesses. "Illinois Capital in Hands of a Raving Mob," blared the paper's headline.[20] In 1917, Fisher Brooks, a black taxi driver in Mobile, Alabama, reportedly robbed and murdered a white passenger, Julia May Hess. After authorities arrested the alleged assailant and brought him to trial "without delay, an all-white jury sentenced him to death by hanging.[21]

But the *Nashville Globe* was not a gloom-and-doom paper; it contained numerous stories of black success and black pride. D. A. Hart, the paper's managing editor, balanced horror stories of racial atrocities with accounts of hope and heroism. The black leader most celebrated in the Nashville paper was, without question, Booker T. Washington. A former enslaved person from Virginia and educated at the Hampton Agricultural and Industrial School (now Hampton University), he rose to national prominence with his "Atlanta Exposition" speech in 1895. Many white and black Southerners admired Washington, and the citizens of Nashville were no different. The editor of the *Nashville Globe* called him a "prime favorite with all the people of Nashville."[22] Dubbed the "Wizard of Tuskegee," the paper added that Washington was known on "every continent and loved by the Nashville people." Indeed, Washington was a member of the board of trustees at Fisk University from 1909 until his death in 1915.[23]

On one hand, white Southerners lauded Washington because he openly denounced "social equality" and championed the cause of industrial education. On the other, black Southerners commended his emphasis on entrepreneurship among African Americans and his voice of optimism. After the Alabama educator visited Nashville

---

[20] "Reign of Terror," *Nashville Globe* (August 21, 1908): 1, 5. The Springfield Race Riot, which took place on August 14–16, 1908 in the adopted hometown of Abraham Lincoln, precipitated the founding of the National Association for the Advancement of Colored People (NAACP) by W. E. B. Du Bois and others. See John Hope Franklin and Evelyn Brooks Higginbotham, *From Slavery to Freedom: A History of African Americans* (9th ed.) (New York: McGraw, 1947/2011), 286.

[21] "Negro Man Must Die," *Nashville Globe* (July 6, 1917): 7.

[22] "Booker Washington Coming," *Nashville Globe* (March 1, 1907): 2.

[23] "Vernon-Washington Banquet," *Nashville Globe* (April 13, 1908): 2. Louis R. Harlan, *Booker T. Washington: The Wizard of Tuskegee, 1901–1915* (New York: Oxford University Press, 1983), 181.

in the spring of 1907, the *Nashville Globe* observed, "The doctrine of optimism is the doctrine of hopefulness, and this was never more forcibly preached to the race than was done by one of its most powerful leaders, Booker T. Washington."[24]

Preston Taylor and other African American dignitaries wined and dined with Washington when he traveled to Middle Tennessee. They admired him, and the Tuskegee leader appreciated them, especially Taylor. In his book *The Negro in Business*, Washington singled out the Nashville businessman for special recognition: "Rev. Preston Taylor, who early in life learned a trade, has been a contractor, assistant baggage-master as well as preacher, and has finally become comfortably well off in the business of undertaking." Washington applauded Taylor as a "safe and wise business man."[25] In Washington's view, Taylor stood shoulders above the other African American leaders because he was multitalented and wielded far-reaching influence in Middle Tennessee and beyond.

The *Globe* also commended the literary achievements of Paul Laurence Dunbar, the "world's greatest Negro poet."[26] The paper advertised that Taylor's Greenwood Park would provide "Telegraphic Detail" of the Jack Johnson and Jim Jefferies fight; it then relished in Johnson's triumph over the white contender, declaring on its front page that the black heavyweight champion "*easily disposes of Jim Jeffries*," with "only fifteen rounds to do the trick."[27] The *Globe*'s sporting news page kept fans apprised of the success of Major Taylor, an African American world cycling champion. Nicknamed the "Colored Whirlwind," Taylor vanquished cycling opponents in America and Europe.[28]

In the summer of 1908, the National Baptist Publishing Board (NBPB) in Nashville started making dolls and marketing them to the African American community. The *Nashville Globe* announced that African Americans "now want their girl children to have something

---

[24] "A Tribute of Respect to Washington," *Nashville Globe* (April 15, 1907): 4.

[25] Washington, *The Negro in Business*, 102.

[26] "Paul Laurence Dunbar," *Nashville Globe* (June 14, 1907): 4.

[27] For an advertisement of the Johnson-Jefferies fight, see "Exclusively for Negroes!" *Nashville Globe* (May 27, 1910): 2. "Smiling Jack," *Nashville Globe* (July 8, 1910): 1.

[28] "The World's Famous Bicycle Rider Again on the Track," *Nashville Globe* (July 19, 1907): 8. "Sporting News," *Nashville Globe* (March 20, 1908): 8.

that will come nearer representing the race. Many of them have declared that if they could get a colored doll to give their child they would do so. The opportunity is now offered."²⁹ The promotion of black dolls coincided with the advertisement of hair and beauty products for black women. In September of 1913, the *Nashville Globe* announced that Madam C. J. Walker, the renowned hair culturalist, was coming to the city. The local paper billed her as "one of the most progressive women of the race. Wherever she goes she sows seeds of inspiration and enterprise."³⁰

The tales of Booker T. Washington, Paul Laurence Dunbar, Jack Johnson, Major Taylor, Madam C. J. Walker, and others provided black readers and residents in Middle Tennessee with glimmers of hope and reasons to boast in a virulent racist and anti-black society. The rise of these African Americans from poverty to prominence stirred dreams of opportunity and visions of confidence. Indeed, the "doctrine of optimism," which Booker T. Washington espoused and proclaimed, animated the spirit of Preston Taylor, who toiled to pave the way for his people in Middle Tennessee and beyond.

A Tour of the South

When Taylor embarked on a tour of the Deep South in 1907, he exuded an ethos of optimism. In Birmingham, Alabama, he witnessed black laborers on the railroads and in the coal mines. Known as the "Pittsburgh of the South," Taylor called it "magnetic, and our people are well established along all walks of life; they own good homes and many of them are beautiful places of great value." The Penny Savings Bank, the Bond & Company (a clothing store for black men), the funeral home, and the Mason Building, which housed a large and well-organized pharmacy as well as an insurance company, all impressed the visitor from Nashville, prompting him to conclude, "Birmingham has her share of professional men, such as lawyers, doctors, etc., and will rank with any city in the country. Our race is well cared for in the post office and the city government."³¹

---

²⁹ "Colored Dolls for Christmas," *Nashville Globe* (July 31, 1908): 6. "Dolls, Dolls, Negro Dolls," *Nashville Globe* (August 28, 1908): 8. "Your Doll Is Now Ready," *Nashville Globe* (October 30, 1908): 8.

³⁰ "Madam C. J. Walker Coming," *Nashville Globe* (September 5, 1913): 4. "Mrs. Walker Coming to Nashville," *Nashville Globe* (September 19, 1913): 6.

³¹ Preston Taylor, "Southern Trip" *Nashville Globe* (February 1, 1907): 6.

From Birmingham, Taylor made his way to St. Augustine, Florida. Along the five-hundred-mile excursion from the Magic City to the Ancient City, four things struck Taylor. First, he noticed no "loafers" hanging around railroad depots. "Any number of ebony faces could constantly be seen all along the entire route, but they were employed in different vocations." Taylor used the tour to prod black Nashvillians to take full advantage of labor opportunities. "Let our race prove loyal to the call," he admonished, "and prove ourselves worthy of the confidence imposed in us; do a day's work for a day's pay, and give no opportunity to have the country filled with foreign emigrants to supplant the race who has made the country what it is today."[32]

Next, while traveling through Alabama, he saw black laborers tapping tall pine trees for rosin and hauling it to the refinery, while others were busily converting large forests into lumber to be sent "all over the world." Third, as a former railroad porter, Taylor especially delighted in seeing African American men covering the railroad industry. "The man of ebony," he chuckled, "is a natural railroad man, and we noted him occupying all the positions along the line, such as brakeman, fireman, section man, etc. One night the conductor went to sleep and our ebony porter was in charge."[33]

Fourth, when crossing over into the Florida border, Taylor noticed a dramatic change in the temperature, from the cold and ice in Alabama to "warm, balmy summer-like weather" in the Sunshine State. Indeed, when Taylor and R. E. Watkins arrived in St. Augustine, they said, "Is this next to heaven? For surely this city is a paradise, with streets white and smooth with coral and sand." Yet he was even more impressed that black people owned top-quality restaurants and boarding houses. In the oldest continuous U.S. city, Taylor found African Americans "employed as salesmen in the stores; they are the most reliable guides and the best-informed people on most subjects as to the old landmarks."[34]

According to Taylor, Daytona Beach, Florida, fifty-five miles south of St. Augustine, lived up to its reputation of having the "most beautiful sea beach in the world." Taylor and Watkins stayed with J. C. M. Combs, a local preacher who had purchased a "block in Daytona" for $1,500 and he refused to take $10,000 for it "while we were in

---

[32] Preston Taylor, "Southern Trip" *Nashville Globe* (February 22, 1907): 3.
[33] Ibid.
[34] Ibid.

his city." Black Floridians owned and grew orange trees, pineapple trees, coconut trees, and banana trees—"precious fruit," which they "ship all over the world." After learning that Daytona Beach had only two police officers because of low crime and "no saloons," Taylor exclaimed, "What a heaven on earth to live in such a country like this! Don't you want to go there?"[35]

On his way back to Nashville, Taylor stopped in Tuskegee, Alabama. In his comments of his tour of the Tuskegee campus, he disclosed his philosophy of race and education, asserting,

> If the brother in black is ignorant, his shadow falls on his white brother and God has made of one blood all nations though his skin may be white, black or red and yet the same blood unchanged and what is the interest of one man must be the welfare of all. From the time the Emancipation Proclamation was put in force until believed to be the best money a parent can spend on his children.[36]

Taylor took seriously the biblical text, Acts 17:28, which established and cemented for him the equality of all human beings, and he felt personally the impact of the Emancipation Proclamation that, although not "freeing" enslaved people in the Border State of Kentucky, led to the recruitment of black soldiers into the Union Army.

The eighty buildings standing on 2,300 acres of land—along with the industrious students, who built furniture, made clothing, and manicured gardens and greenhouses—inspired Taylor. In his view, a liberal arts education and manual training complemented each other. He wrote of the place:

> [Tuskegee's] constant aim is to correlate the literary and industrial training that the student cannot get one without the other; hence the students go to school one day and the next day he works at his trade and still to accommodate all, the school is operated day and night. You never find an idler in Tuskegee; every hour must be accounted for. There is a great demand for the Tuskegee graduates.

---

[35] Ibid.
[36] Preston Taylor, "Southern Trip" *Nashville Globe* (March 1, 1907): 3.

Taylor lamented that the misdeeds of black people often garnered more publicity than their good works, and he concluded: "If the world could only know what Tuskegee is doing for the uplifting of humanity, we would be willing to rest our case with them."[37]

Upon returning to Nashville, Taylor had much to reflect on from what he saw during his trip across the Deep South. Without question, the burgeoning progress of black Southerners as land and business owners solidified his belief in the "doctrine of optimism." More significantly, what Booker T. Washington endeavored to do for young African Americans in Alabama at the Tuskegee Institute and for black people generally in the National Negro Business League (NNBL), Taylor toiled to do in his efforts as a church leader, funeral director, and civic leader in Middle Tennessee and beyond.

'The Negro Cannot Be a Democrat'

Precipitated by the Brownsville Race Riot, the subject of politics and race saturated the pages of the *Nashville Globe* in the summer of 1906, when African American soldiers of the 25th Regiment, stationed in Brownsville, Texas, became embroiled in racial conflict, that resulted in one dead resident, another wounded, and the police chief injured. After reports circulated that black soldiers had "shot up the town," racial hostility boiled over in the south Texas community. Based on a false report that black soldiers deliberately maimed and murdered several Brownsville citizens, President Theodore Roosevelt dismissed the entire battalion without honor and barred them from future military service and civil positions in the United States government.[38] Historian H. W. Brands has observed that the American press "refought the Civil War over the Brownsville incident," adding, "Among those drummed out of the army in Roosevelt's summary judgment were several winners of the Medal of Honor; this circumstance underscored what many believed was unfair and thoroughly un-American imputation of guilt by association."[39]

---

[37] Ibid.
[38] Franklin and Higginbotham, *From Slavery to Freedom*, 284–285.
[39] H. W. Brands, *T. R.: The Last Romantic* (New York: Basic Books, 1997), 588.

The *Nashville Globe* followed the Brownsville Affair closely and called the president's decision "an outrage."⁴⁰ The black newspaper heaped enormous praise upon Joseph B. Foraker, a Republican senator from Ohio who openly denounced the Senate committee that upheld Roosevelt's verdict. The same paper noted that, during the 1908 U.S. presidential election between Republican candidate William H. Taft and Democratic nominee William Jennings Bryan, the Brownsville Affair surfaced as a political issue. Bryan's statement that the south Texas episode was handled improperly prompted the *Globe* to observe that the black man in 1908 is "going to vote for the best man. Whether that vote shall be for Taft or Bryan will depend very much upon how these men shall express themselves upon questions vital to the Negro, during the campaign."⁴¹

Indeed, on August 31, 1908, the St. John African Methodist Episcopal Church in Nashville hosted a debate between lawyer R. L. Mayfield and attorney A. N. Johnson. The African American leaders discussed this question: "Should the Negro support W. J. Bryan, the Democratic Nominee, or W. H. Taft, the Republican Nominee, for the presidency?"⁴² The *Globe* deemed the debate highly relevant and significant in light of the recent race riot in Springfield, Illinois, and the looming presidential election. On the night of the debate, which lasted from 8:30 PM to 11:10 PM, the paper pointed out that, on the one hand, Mayfield seemed unprepared and made "weak" arguments. On the other hand, Johnson "made decidedly the best argument." Arguing that the Republican Party, organized in 1854, was "dedicated to the great principle that all men are and ought to be free and equal," Johnson poignantly stated, "The Democratic party is a party of slavery," highlighting that Georgia politician Robert Toombs, "proclaimed that he should one day stand upon the hallowed spot where Crispus Attucks fell—at the foot of Bunker Hill—and sell

---

⁴⁰ "An Embarrassing Issue," *Nashville Globe* (July 17, 1908):4.

⁴¹ "The Negro Voter," *Nashville Globe* (August 14, 1908): 4. Michael Kazin, *A Godly Hero: The Life of William Jennings Bryan* (New York: Alfred A. Knopf, 2006), 161. Kazin observed that African American leader W. E. B. Du Bois (1868–1963) said that it was time for a change, stating, "But I shall vote for Bryan."

⁴² "All Thinking Negroes," *Nashville Globe* (August 14, 1908): 8. See also, "The Springfield Riot, Bloody Deed Dreadful," *Nashville Globe* (August 21, 1908): 3.

slaves to the highest bidder." Thus, Johnson concluded, "The Negro cannot be a Democrat."[43]

Without a doubt, Preston Taylor was in the audience that night. Even though he never publicly disclosed his political affiliation, Taylor, like most of the black establishment in Middle Tennessee, supported the party of Lincoln. The debate attests to just how closely political and racial issues were intertwined. In fact, by supporting the Republican ticket, Johnson, Taylor, and other African Americans believed they were simultaneously fighting the devil, the enemy of racial justice. In the 1930s, under the influence of the New Deal, African Americans began shifting in large numbers from the Republican Party to the Democratic fold. This political transitioning gained more steam in the 1960s; today, the overwhelming majority of black people support the Democratic Party.

Embracing the Poor, the Cold, and the Hungry

In the winter of 1910, Taylor continued to promote the doctrine of optimism, and he collaborated with other black civic and religious leaders to organize the Helping Hand Variety Store for the "purpose of relieving the poor and destitute." On the day the store formally opened, Taylor gave the keynote address and compared the new store to Tremont Hall in Boston, Massachusetts, "where everything wanted could be had," that the "man who worked for the uplift of the people would succeed. He cited several instances where Negroes have started business on a small scale and had carried the same to great success." The *Nashville Globe* reported that African Americans often waited to see the "outcome" of a black business, but Taylor poignantly stated, "But do you know that anything will die unless you patronize it?"[44] Taylor clearly understood the value of black people supporting their own enterprises in their own communities.

The following year, African American leaders in Nashville again reached across denominational lines and collaborated to organize a "Men and Religion Movement." The committee of fifty men, with subcommittees, chose Pastor W. S. Ellington to chair the evangelism program. Professor G. E. Haynes presided over

---

[43] "Great Debate, One Sided Affair," *Nashville Globe* (September 4, 1908): 1, 7.

[44] "Variety Store Opens Next Tuesday," *Nashville Globe* (January 28, 1910): 1. "Opening of the Helping Hand Variety Store," *Nashville Globe* (February 4, 1910): 1.

the social service department. Professor Hardy Keith oversaw the boys' work committee, while Professor J. W. Work led the publicity unit. Preston Taylor chaired the conservation section. The leaders hoped that "hundreds of men who are not now interested in the church of God, will be converted and turned into willing workers for the building up of the Kingdom."[45] This ecumenical organization intentionally worked to help bring about spiritual renewal and spiritual transformation in black Nashville.

For Taylor, however, building up the kingdom of God meant more than saving souls; it also meant addressing the material, physical, and social needs of his people. Two months after the launching of the "Men and Religion Movement," meteorologists warned Nashvillians about impending frigid temperatures, announcing, "Zero weather is an unwelcome tip for the residents of this city, but the weather man has so ordered and we must stand for it." The forecasters were right, as subfreezing temperatures saturated Middle Tennessee and Nashville's lower classes felt the pain. "A sick man, his hungry wife, and child seated around a flickering lamp to keep warm," a local reporter said, "was a sight which greeted some of the workers of the United Charities when they entered a tenement in Nashville."[46]

The bitterly cold weather blast killed humans and animals alike. D. H. Kirby, a seventy-year-old Confederate veteran, lived alone and was found near death either by paralysis or by "exposure from the cold." In Columbia, Tennessee, hundreds of lambs and pigs froze to death. The cold weather hampered the shipment of fruits and vegetables, thereby hurting the pocketbooks of Nashville merchants. The *Tennessean* lamented, "Nashville jobbers are still tied up on account of the cold weather."[47]

The icy-cold conditions forced many Nashville residents to apply for assistance with coal and clothing. Mayor Hilary Ewing Howse, who was out of town when the artic blast hit Middle Tennessee, issued an order that "despite the fact that the money is nearly out of the coal fund, at least a thousand bushels of coal be given out to

---

[45] "Men and Religion Movement," *Nashville Globe* (November 17, 1911): 5.

[46] "Zero Weather Is an Unwelcome Tip," *The Tennessean* (January 7, 1912): 38. "Nashville Poor Hard Hit by this Bitter Weather," *The Tennessean* (January 8, 1912): 3.

[47] "Found Dying in Solitude," *The Tennessean* (January 10, 1912): 2. "Cold Kills Animals," *The Tennessean* (January 11, 1912): 9. "Fruits and Vegetables," *The Tennessean* (January 11, 1912): 19.

those applying for aid." The mayor's order, the *Tennessean* reported, "probably saved much suffering, as many of those applying for aid Monday were in absolute and immediate need of supplies. In many of the cases the children were suffering from want of heat."[48]

The severe cold temperatures prompted Dr. J. E. McCulloch, chairman of the Social Service Committee for Protestant Churches, to appeal to congregations across Nashville to open their "well heated" buildings to alleviate the "suffering poor" and to "shelter those who are without homes."[49]

Preston Taylor was one of many religious leaders who came to the aid of impoverished black Nashvillians affected by the frigid weather. Fannie Battle, a coordinator with United Charities in Middle Tennessee, announced that Taylor generously offered the use of a "large and comfortable hall." Battle added, "This hall is well heated and fires will be kept up day and night. Hot soup and coffee are prepared by the United Charity workers and all colored people who are cold and hungry will find a welcome." The coordinator expressed great pleasure at Taylor's generosity and hospitality, as "much difficulty has been experienced in caring for the colored sufferers."[50]

It is unclear whether white congregations opened their facilities to their destitute black neighbors. David Lipscomb was a true champion of the poor, and he urged white Christians to welcome black people into their churches. In 1907, he upbraided white believers who complained when Mr. and Mrs. Elam brought a little black girl to their worship service at the Bellwood Church of Christ in Nashville, stating, "To object to any child of God participating in the services on account of his race, social or civil state, his color or race, is to object to Jesus Christ and to cast him from our association. It is a fearful thing to do."[51]

---

[48] "Many Apply at City Hall for Coal and Help," *The Tennessean* (January 9, 1912): 3.

[49] "Requests Churches to Open to Alleviate Suffering," *The Tennessean* (January 8, 1912): 11.

[50] "Provision for the Colored Sufferers," *The Tennessean* (January 16, 1912): 11.

[51] David Lipscomb, "The Negro in Worship—A Correspondence," *Gospel Advocate* 49 (July 4, 1907): 425. See also, Richard T. Hughes, *Reviving the Ancient Faith: The Story of Churches of Christ in America* (Abilene, TX: Abilene Christian University Press, 1996/2008), 272-273. Harold Shank, "Nashville's Central Church of Christ: The First Twenty Years," *Restoration Quarterly* 41 (1999): 11-26. Shank has also shown that, from 1925 to 1945, Nashville's Central Church of Christ had robust evangelism and benevolence ministries.

In spite of Lipscomb's plea, author Elizabeth K. Goetsch has observed that rigid segregation "plagued Nashville," adding, "blacks did not dine with whites, blacks were not supposed to touch whites and so on. White Nashvillians tried to justify these actions by equating skin color with poverty and poverty with bad behavior."[52]

Notwithstanding Nashville's racial divide, Taylor clearly took the lead in offering assistance to his people, African Americans. Furthermore, his generous actions confirm that he took seriously the teachings of Jesus about feeding the hungry, clothing the naked, and welcoming the stranger in Matthew 25; he also took to heart the practical tenets of James about assisting people with "those things that are needful to the body" (James 2:15–16). Preston Taylor, then, was a "doer of the word."

In a complex and tumultuous world swirling with racial violence, white supremacy, and distorted literary and cinematic images of black people, African American civic and church leaders collaborated to "fight the devil" in Middle Tennessee. Taylor was clearly a leader in this fight, as head of the United Transportation Company, as a proponent of the "doctrine of optimism," and as a champion of black pride. He understood that African Americans could not always depend on their white neighbors to help them; therefore, they had to apply "elbow grease" and help themselves. Just as he had done two decades earlier, when he calmly stepped forward and comforted a bereaved community when three firefighters fell, he achieved a similar feat during the winter storm of 1912. When shivering and destitute black people needed food, clothing, and shelter, Taylor looked out for his fellow African Americans. This was his way of "fighting the devil in Nashville" and paving the way for his people.

---

[52] Elizabeth K. Goetsch, *Wicked Nashville* (Charleston, SC: The History Press, 2017), 83.

Six

A Resting Place and a Breathing Place

The Formation of Greenwood Cemetery and Greenwood Park

Let everything that hath breath, Praise the Lord.
—Psalm 150:1

As I bear my neighbor's burden,
And I stagger 'neath its weight,
I'm beset with dire foreboding
Lest a fall should be my fate.

And I ask, why should I worry
With the troubles of another?
Then the answer comes with hurry,
"He aint heavy, he's my brother.[1]
—Micah S. Combs

When Taylor transitioned from Mt. Sterling, Kentucky, to Nashville, Tennessee, the 1883 U.S. Supreme Court had declared unconstitutional the Civil Rights Act of 1875, which had guaranteed African Americans' rights to use public accommodations freely. The 1883 ruling presaged the *Plessy v. Ferguson* (1896) decision,

---

[1] Micah S. Combs, "He's My Brother," in The Micah S. Combs, Jr. File at the Disciples of Christ Historical Society (DCHS) in Bethany, West Virginia. Many, many thanks to Shelley Jacobs for sharing this information with me.

which legalized segregation, another form of chattel enslavement.[2] As scholars John Hope Franklin and Evelyn Brooks Higginbotham asserted: "In the segregated South, 'we the people' as the polity and citizenry did not include African Americans. Indeed, white southerners frequently referred to America itself as the 'white man's country.'"[3]

Racial violence accompanied *de jure* segregation as, between 1882 and 1903, almost two thousand black people were lynched in the South. Historian Howard N. Rabinowitz has argued that mob violence against African Americans was "employed as a social-control device to keep blacks 'in their place' following real or imagined examples of black social, political, or economic 'uppityness.'"[4]

Notwithstanding this racially charged context, Taylor met a white man, Micah S. Combs, Jr., who changed the trajectory of his future business life. Combs grew up in the Christian Church in Nashville, Tennessee, where his father, Micah Combs, Sr., established a funeral home in 1872. Standing six feet tall and weighing two hundred pounds, Micah, Jr., was known for his cordial and friendly disposition. He befriended and mentored Taylor in the undertaking business shortly after the latter arrived in the city. Micah Combs, Jr., eventually took over his father's funeral business in 1910, and he helped organize the Tennessee Funeral Directors Association and held state embalming license No. 1.[5]

More than a kind funeral director, Combs preached for the Bellevue Christian Church in Nashville for several years, while also writing poetry. His most popular poem, "He's My Brother," was inspired by his encounter with a nine-year-old boy carrying a big fat baby at their mother's funeral. Concerned by what he saw, Combs asked the boy, "Son, isn't that baby pretty heavy?" The adolescent

---

[2] Martin Luther King, Jr., *Strength to Love* (Philadelphia: Fortress Press, 1963/1981), 42.

[3] John Hope Franklin and Evelyn Brooks Higginbotham, *From Slavery to Freedom: A History of African Americans* (9th ed.) (New York: McGraw-Hill, 1947/2011), 247.

[4] Howard N. Rabinowitz, *The First New South, 1865–1920* (Arlington Heights, IL: Harlan Davidson, 1992), 141–142. Some 212 miles west in Memphis, Tennessee, Ida B. Wells (1862–1931) witnessed the lynching of one of her "best friends," Tom Moss, along with his business partners, Calvin McDowell and Will Stewart. See Linda O. McMurry, *To Keep the Waters Troubled: The Life of Ida B. Wells* (New York: Oxford University Press, 1998), 134–135.

[5] Micah S. Combs, Jr. File (DCHS).

replied, "He ain't heavy; he's my brother." The second stanza of the poem went:

> If I can't help my fellow man,
> When he is down and out,
> If I do not do all I can
> To help him get about
> When he is lame and crippled up,
> Why should I care to bother?
> The same God hath made both of us,
> "He ain't heavy, he's my brother."[6]

For Micah S. Combs, Jr., these lines were more than a sentimental story with words of rhyme. He lived out those words and reached across racial boundaries to teach and mentor Preston Taylor, who, in 1888, opened Taylor and Company Undertakers in Nashville. The following year, Taylor purchased land on Elm Hill Pike on a white dairy farm called Buttermilk Ridge and established the Greenwood Cemetery.[7]

Taylor gained city-wide acclaim in 1892, when the three African American firefighters profiled earlier—Charles C. Gowdy, Hardy Ewing, and Stokely H. Allen—perished in a ravishing fire in Nashville. He emerged as a bright and shining light and helped lead a grief-stricken city to a state of comfort and tranquility. As historian Bobby L. Lovett noted,

> By 1892, Taylor and Company Undertakers had become Nashville's largest and most prestigious funeral home, gaining even more publicity in 1892 when it took charge of the public funeral for the three black firemen who lost their lives in a downtown fire. Taylor constructed an ingenious carriage to carry the firemen's bodies side by side during the public funeral processional.[8]

---

[6] Ibid. John Fetterman, "'He's My Brother!' A Nashvillian Penned the Line," *Nashville Tennessee Magazine* (June 19, 1955): 18. Father Edward Flanagan (1886-1948) established Boys Town in 1917 in Omaha, Nebraska, as an orphanage for neglected boys, and he adopted the poem as the slogan for his work in his home state.

[7] Bobby L. Lovett, *The African-American History of Nashville, Tennessee, 1780-1930* (Fayetteville, AR: University of Arkansas Press, 1999), 109.

[8] Ibid.

The conflagration of 1892 helped cement Taylor's influence and renown as an entrepreneur and community leader in the city of Nashville and beyond.

In some ways, Taylor's life embodied the message of Micah Combs's poem, "He's My Brother." The third stanza reads:

> And when I see my fellow man
> In throes of deep distress,
> I'd put my arms around him,
> Whisper words of tenderness,
> And try to chase his gloom away,
> His tears attempt to smother,
> And turn his darkness into day,
> That fellow is my brother.[9]

"He Saw the Need"

In 1908, the *Nashville Globe* celebrated Preston Taylor as a "Nashville Pioneer" for his formation of Greenwood Cemetery and Greenwood Park. The paper boasted,

> Greenwood Cemetery is one the greatest achievements of Mr. Taylor. The colored people had only one cemetery, and that was becoming very crowded. He saw the need and found the remedy, and as a result the Negroes of Nashville can boast of having the most beautifully arranged and the best kept cemetery in this vicinity.

Immaculately groomed and meticulously manicured by Taylor's employees, the paper added, "One does not feel that he is among the dead when in Greenwood Cemetery."[10]

Myriads of African Americans had their remains interred at Greenwood Cemetery. Regardless of how black people passed away or how young or old they were, Taylor and his funeral company often embalmed the body and laid it to rest. When A. G. Caruthers,

---

[9] Micah S. Combs, Jr. File (DCHS).
[10] "A Nashville Pioneer," *Nashville Globe* (September 4, 1908): 15. In 1869, the Colored Sons of Relief Number One and the Colored Benevolent Society opened Nashville's first black cemetery, Mount Ararat Cemetery. See Bobby L. Lovett (ed.), "From Winter to Winter: Afro-American History of Nashville, Tennessee, 1870–1930" (unpublished manuscript, 1981), 17. See also, Tommie Morton-Young, *Nashville, Tennessee: Black America Series* (Charleston, SC: Arcadia Press, 2000), 86.

a black resident of Nashville, jumped into the Cumberland River and committed suicide, Mr. Sanday, a truck gardener, recovered Caruthers's body, the *Globe* reported: "A telephone message was immediately sent to Mr. J. B. Kennedy, another to Taylor & Co., and to the family of the deceased, whereupon preparations were begun to bring the remains into the city. This was done and the remains were carried to Taylor & Company's undertaking establishment."[11]

In the spring of 1907, Nettie Green fatally shot Margaret Gooch; the former then took her own life by "drinking carbolic acid." The two women were romantically involved with Bill Tate. "The remains of Margaret Gooch," the *Globe* noted, "were taken to the undertaking establishment of Taylor & Co."[12]

Professor Arthur D. Langston, a brother-in-law of Nashville lawyer James C. Napier, died in St. Louis, Missouri, but his family chose to bring his body to the Taylor & Company in Nashville, "where the body lay in state all day and was viewed by a host of sorrowing friends. The interment was made in the Napier lot at Greenwood Cemetery."[13]

Henry Bradford, born in 1807 and having passed through the "darkest days of slavery," died at the age of one hundred. His obituary stated that he was "personally acquainted" with Presidents Andrew Jackson, James K. Polk, and "others who made the Volunteer State famous." He fathered eleven children, three of whom reached adulthood. The *Globe* announced, "The Interment was made at Greenwood Cemetery. The funeral was directed by Taylor & Co., only the family and intimate friends being present."[14]

Scholars of the African American funeral industry have keenly observed that the exclusion of black bodies from white cemeteries necessitated the creation of black funeral homes and cemeteries. Historian Suzanne E. Smith has argued that, in response to segregation laws, "many African American funeral directors were working to establish black-owned-and-operated cemeteries to secure a dignified burial ground for their respective communities," adding, "Perhaps no one person better exemplifies the way black funeral directors used their capital and prestige as local community

---

[11] "A. G. Caruthers' Body Recovered," *Nashville Globe* (March 29, 1907): 1.
[12] "Double Tragedy Sunday," *Nashville Globe* (March 29, 1907): 4.
[13] "Interred in Nashville," *Nashville Globe* (May 1, 1908): 3.
[14] "Death of Henry Bradford," *Nashville Globe* (August 7, 1908): 2.

leaders to fight the indignities of racial segregation at the turn of the century than the Reverend Preston Taylor of Nashville, Tennessee."[15]

African Americans funerals made a statement that the lives of black people mattered. As scholar Karla F. C. Holloway observed,

> For many it was important to note the procession of cars and prominent numbers of mourners. Their visual excess expressed a story that African Americans otherwise had difficulty illustrating—that these were lives of importance and substance, or that these were individuals, no matter their failings or the degree to which their lives were quietly lived, who were loved.[16]

In the mind of Preston Taylor, the lives of African Americans mattered both in life and in death.

A Breathing Place

Not only did Taylor display kindness to the deceased, he also wanted black people living in Middle Tennessee to enjoy life, leisure, and laughter. Racial discrimination excluded African Americans from public parks across the Jim Crow South. In white Southern thought, black people lacked self-control and represented, in the words of historian Ted Ownby, the "depths of savagery." Therefore, white lawmakers in the segregated South, to "protect the purity of white women," barred their black counterparts from parks and recreational facilities.[17]

Knowing that fellow African Americans were bereft of leisure and amusement spaces in the South, Taylor created Greenwood Park around 1904 in Nashville, to offer social, emotional, physical, and moral uplift. The park contained multiple attractions: a barbecue stand, a bandstand, baseball stadiums, gardens, a lunchroom, a picnic area, an old plantation scene, a merry-go-round, a lunchroom, a roller coaster, a skating rink, a theater, a shooting gallery, and side

---

[15] Suzanne E. Smith, *To Serve the Living: Funeral Directors and the American Way of Death* (Cambridge, MA: Belknap Press of Harvard University, 2010), 57, 59.

[16] Karla F. C. Holloway, *Passed On: African American Mourning Stories* (Durham, NC: Duke University Press, 2002), 181.

[17] Ted Ownby, *Subduing Satan: Religion, Recreation, and Manhood in the Rural South, 1865–1920* (Chapel Hill, NC: University of North Carolina Press, 1990), 16, 117.

shows.[18] From Taylor's perspective, Greenwood Park provided black Nashvillians opportunities for fun, frolic, and freedom from white harassment and oppression.

A few years after Greenwood Park opened, however, the Tennessee State Legislature voted to close the facility, citing that places of recreation could not operate within two miles of a cemetery. The *Nashville Globe* vigorously assailed the new law and simultaneously explained what Taylor's recreational park meant to black residents. "The passage of the bill," the paper asserted, "blotted out the only breathing place where the colored citizens of this place could go to get out of the dust, grime and foul gases of the city and get a little fresh air and enjoy themselves," noting, "It was a gerrymander of the worst kind."[19]

Because the new legislation did not affect white amusement parks, black locals deemed the code racist. The *Globe* expounded,

> [African Americans] have been shut out from the parks and places of amusements frequented by the white race, and they are forbidden by a law to have one and the one they have is struck down by this unwarranted act. The class behind this law admits by its passage that the Negro must be checked in his progress.[20]

While rebuking the biased legislation and lawmakers, the same paper heaped praise on the architect of Greenwood Park, lauding:

> Greenwood Park is the gift of the Elder Preston Taylor for the free use of his people as a place of amusement. This generous, prosperous, public-spirited man saw the need of such a refining influence for his people and his great heart went out to them to the extent of this magnificent gift which to them cannot be measured by dollars and cents, though it cost him twenty thousand dollars to put it into its present condition.

The paper then compared the action of Davidson's County statesmen to the treachery of King David, who struck down Uriah and confiscated his wife, Bathsheba, even though David already had multiple wives.[21]

---

[18] Lovett, *The African-American History*, 123.
[19] "Beautiful Greenwood Park," *Nashville Globe* (April 12, 1907): 1.
[20] Ibid.
[21] Ibid.

A week after the Tennessee Legislature passed the "iniquitous Park Bill," Governor Malcolm Rice Patterson vetoed the law, prompting black people in Nashville to cheer: "In withholding his approval to the scheme he put his foot down hard upon the copper-headed prejudice which would use the legislature for the purpose of striking at the rights of the colored people to enjoy themselves under their own vine and fig tree."

The *Nashville Globe* again explained the significance of Greenwood Park, arguing that white leaders in the Volunteer State,

> emphasized so forcibly that Negroes are not admitted at their private parks and no self-respecting person of our race wants to visit them—they have shown so plainly that even at the parks owned by the city that we are not wanted, and we thought surely they would be consistent enough to let us alone when one of our public-men threw open a breathing place where we could escape from the miasma of those sections of the city where most of our people live.[22]

African Americans in the city of Nashville, then, needed Greenwood Park for two reasons: First, black residents were not welcomed at white parks; second, they yearned for a place and space to exhale and "breathe" freely from white harassment and domination.

Indeed, on Independence Day of 1907, black residents got a chance to exhale, as Greenwood Park was full of "throngs of people" with "teeming thousands." "Everybody seemed bent on getting all that was coming in the way of pleasure and enjoyment," the *Globe* reported. Preachers and their congregants joined in the festive activities and filled the skating rink with "merry skaters"; and the merry-go-round had "hundreds and hundreds of pastors and spectators." The appearance of three white concession workers, however, upset black attendees, who "emphatically objected to the presence of these men under any circumstances." A writer for the *Globe* asked Taylor, "was it the intention of the management to countenance the presence of white men by selling them concessions?" The park's founder answered that black men, "without his knowledge," let the white participants in. Taylor then stated, "Please say for me that Greenwood Park is owned by colored people, run by colored people for colored people."[23]

---

[22] "Greenwood Park," *Nashville Globe* (April 19, 1907): 4.
[23] "Fourth of July at Greenwood Park," *Nashville Globe* (July 12, 1907): 2.

Taylor constructed Greenwood Park to advocate for black pride and to showcase black progress. It was indeed a commercial enterprise, but historian Bobby L. Lovett observed that Taylor's park served as a tool to "influence the behavior of ordinary blacks"; and it "operated with order and dignity; his large home was there; and he did not allow cursing, drinking, or fighting in Greenwood Park. The patrons had to dress up and act with good manners."[24]

Greenwood Park served as host to many important community events for African Americans. In the spring of 1907, Nashville's black Baptists brought together thirty-one Sunday schools to provide moral and biblical instruction.[25] A short time later, two Baptist groups held picnics at the popular park. The *Nashville Globe* reported: "Groups of picnickers were scattered here and there over the park," adding:

> Those who watched the gleeful abandon of the children as they enjoyed themselves, whether chasing each other, like the cool zephyrs, across the grassy stretches of the park or disporting themselves upon the wooden horses of the merry-go-round—the older ones who saw all of this innocent joy of the little ones could not but feel its warmth and the spirit of rejuvenance [*sic*].[26]

Greenwood Park was clearly open to all black people of different ages and denominational affiliations.

One of the grandest events hosted at Greenwood Park was the Tennessee State Colored Fair. Organized under the rubric Tennessee Colored Fair Association (TCFA), the group began meeting in December of 1907 with attorney J. C. Napier at its lead. The following month, a woman's department was organized to send invitations to "every woman of every church and every society in the city" to attend the next scheduled meeting on January 25, 1908. Yet when the newly established body was uncertain when to hold the Fair, Taylor gave the organization "all the assurance" he was willing to help in any way to move them forward, stating,

> [T]here will be nothing done on his part to impede the progress or success of the fair, as far as having a place to give

---
[24] Lovett, *The African-American History*, 125.
[25] "Children's Day Celebration," *Nashville Globe* (May 31, 1907): 2.
[26] "Two Enjoyable Picnics," *Nashville Globe* (August 2, 1907): 1.

it, as the grounds of the Greenwood Park were secured for the pleasure and enjoyment, comfort and accommodation of the Negro race at any and all times.[27]

To prepare for the Fair, the *Globe* announced that there were ten thousand cubic yards of dirt to move and asked men with good horses and mules to "apply at once." The advertisement further stated: "Also the plans and specifications for building the fair and Athletic Park are ready, carpenters and lumber men are requested to bid for the work."[28] Preston Taylor clearly understood that the Fair's success depended largely on the physical labor of black men.

At February's meeting, the paper reported that after Taylor "invoked the blessings of God upon the deliberations of the Association," he and the TFCA committee members announced that they were working on a "written contract" for Greenwood Park to host the Fair. Georgia Gordon Taylor, Preston's wife, served as president of the Woman's Department and noted that her group of twenty-five women was "composed of some of the moving spirits of the homes of Nashville, and of the different churches and societies, both secret and benevolent and every walk of life."[29] Indeed, as opening day drew near, the *Nashville Globe* published an article titled, "Nothing Complete Without Them," highlighting the significant contribution of African American women in Middle Tennessee to the launching of their own Fair. The paper asserted,

> Save when there is a feminine side, nothing has ever been thoroughly accomplished, and the Tennessee Colored Fair Association is no exception. The Women's Department of this Association boasts of a large number of energetic and thoroughly interested members and under the direction of its President, Mrs. Preston Taylor, has done a wonderful amount of work.[30]

The TCFA's women's department, according to the *Nashville Globe*, comprised ladies "whose zeal, earnestness and consciousness

---

[27] "Fair Association Meets," *Nashville Globe* (December 13, 1907): 7. "State Fair Association," *Nashville Globe* (January 17, 1908): 1.

[28] "Notice to Contractors," *Nashville Globe* (January 31, 1908): 5.

[29] "Executive Board of Tennessee," *Nashville Globe* (February 14, 1908): 1.

[30] "Nothing Complete Without Them," *Nashville Globe* (August 28, 1908): 1.

of duty have not been and cannot be surpassed by any band of women on the globe. There is no department which comes under a woman's supervision which will not be represented. Everything that the brain, hands and heart of woman can accomplish will be exhibited." The women promised the flakiest breads, cakes, pastries, preserves, wines, and the most transparent jellies. A few weeks before the Fair's opening, the editor of the *Globe* observed, "Already some of the choicest needle work, pyrography, painting, sculpture, millinery and dressmaking are ready."[31]

Just a month after the race riot in Springfield, Illinois, which precipitated the formation of the National Association for the Advancement of Colored People (NAACP), the TCFA boasted that the long-anticipated Fair got off to an "auspicious opening." After a quartette from Fisk University gave a stirring rendition of "Old Kentucky Home," Governor Malcolm R. Patterson helped kick off the festivities with a stirring speech, acknowledging that he was,

> a Southern man, born in a Southern state with all the prejudices of a Southern man, but he was a friend to the Negro so long as he obeyed the law. He, like all true Southerners, wants to help the Negro to better his condition, and he was glad to note the evidence of progress as shown at the fair. God has placed the white man and the black man here ... and it was left for the races to work out their own destiny.

Patterson's oration, saturated with racial and religious overtones, opens a window into race relations in Middle Tennessee in the early twentieth century. In the mind of the governor, black Southerners were acceptable to white Southerners as long as they "obeyed the law"—that is, remained in a "place" of subordination. God's will sanctioned the "place" of whites and blacks in the Jim Crow South. Notwithstanding his covert paternalism and racism, the largely black audience gave him a "hearty applause" when he finished.[32]

The Tennessee State Fair for African Americans came and went in a "blaze of glory," averaging a thousand paid admissions each day. Popular attractions included a horse show with many "fine

---

[31] Ibid.
[32] "First Annual Exhibition," *Nashville Globe* (September 18, 1908): 1.

specimens," band performances, the acrobatic work of the Martin brothers, and some of the finest "livestock ever shown in the state." The women's department did not disappoint with its exhibition of cakes, jellies, preserves, and the like. The *Nashville Globe* commented, "From time immemorial our women have been queens in the culinary and they exhibited their rights to still rule by the samples they had on exhibition." Inspired and buoyed by the support and participation they received, leaders of the TCFA vowed to produce a "bigger, brighter, better show" in 1909.[33]

Taylor organized Greenwood Park not only for black adults; he welcomed children to enjoy amusements as well. In the spring of 1908, the park opened its gates to scores of children for an Easter egg hunt. After Georgia Gordon Taylor, Mrs. Armstrong, and Miss Watkins hid the eggs, the children "could hardly restrain from breaking out of the walls before the door again opened. Finally they were given permission to hunt. Away they went through the tall grass, over the hills in search of the two hundred eggs that had been deposited." Each egg bore the Greenwood Park imprint; seventy contained numbers for a prize; and one gold egg held the prize of $5, which Eugene Hatcher captured. A *Nashville Globe* subtitle read, "Rev. Preston Taylor Children's Best Friend."[34]

Another significant affair at Greenwood Park was "Emancipation Day," which African Americans in Middle Tennessee used to celebrate and commemorate Abraham Lincoln's signing of the Emancipation Proclamation. For black Nashvillians and many other Southern blacks, Abraham Lincoln—not Thomas Jefferson—was their hero. Hence, in the mind of African Americans in the Progressive Era, Independence Day was a time to celebrate their freedom from chattel enslavement, not a time to observe the nation's severance from British tyranny. Preston Taylor took advantage of the first annual Emancipation Day to formally dedicate Greenwood Park. The *Nashville Globe* announced that Taylor, "proprietor of Greenwood Park, that beautiful resort that has added hours of rest and a place of recuperation, has arranged to dedicate the park on that day to the Negroes of Nashville and the state of Tennessee."[35]

---

[33] "First Annual Exhibition," *Nashville Globe* (September 25, 1908): 1.
[34] "Egg Hunt at Greenwood Park," *Nashville Globe* (May 1, 1908): 1.
[35] "Emancipation Celebration," *Nashville Globe* (July 24, 1908): 1.

When promoting the upcoming events for Emancipation Day, the *Nashville Globe* announced Reverend Evans Tyree, a Methodist bishop, as the keynote speaker for the dedication. Additionally, the paper explained why Greenwood Park was a necessity for black Nashvillians. The forty-thousand African Americans in Middle Tennessee had no place to "spend a quiet hour during the hot summer months." White parks posted signs, "Dogs and Niggers Not Allowed," which repelled black residents who wanted to "go somewhere to get a breath of fresh air." Taylor, then, stepped forward and issued a "second emancipation," reported the *Globe*: "Mr. Preston Taylor was not asleep as to the sufferings of his people and though he said nothing he was planning all the time, and as soon as the opportunity came, he took advantage of it, and it was the stroke of his pen that brought the second emancipation to the Negroes of Nashville, and Saturday he has called them to meet at the park and accept the gift that he has labored so arduously to make for his people."

Thousands of black locals attended the Emancipation Day occasion.[36] Greenwood Park was a breathing place for black Nashvillians to enjoy food, fun, frolic, and freedom.

One Sunday evening, January 9, 1910, flames engulfed Greenwood Park and wreaked havoc on the grandstand, which sustained $6,000 in damages. Local white media outlets reported that residents living near the park set it afire out of resentment and opposition to having it in their neighborhood. Taylor, when interviewed by the *Globe*, dismissed the allegations, and he "stated positively" that there was no foul play, explaining,

> [D]uring the years that Greenwood Park had been in existence there has never been a time but when there was some one looking out and searching for some improper act that might be reported to the detriment of the park; but that after all of the diligence and efforts on the part of spotters and sleuths there had not a single case been reported either of gambling or improper conduct on the part of any one that has visited Greenwood Park.

The park's owner called the accusation that white residents started the fire "absolute folly," adding that "cordial relations existed

---

[36] "Record Breaking Crowd," *Nashville Globe* (August 7, 1908): 1.

between the people around the park and himself; that they were always willing to show him a courtesy and he was likewise toward them." The *Globe* used the incident to highlight that as many as 10,000 people had attended Greenwood Park at one time, and that they "come from all sections of the city to enjoy the pleasures that were theirs to enjoy, but all of them at all times conducted themselves in the most orderly manner."[37]

Notwithstanding the partial destruction of Greenwood Park, the pleasure ground continued to play host to a variety of significant events and activities, such as baseball games and boxing matches. In the summer of 1910, the National Baptist Publishing Board held its annual picnic at the park; in the fall, black Nashvillians celebrated the annual state fair. Religious groups and Masonic organizations frequented the facility.[38] For a week, September 9–15, 1918, Taylor and the Lea Avenue Christian Church hosted the second annual National Convention of Colored Churches of Christ at Greenwood Park.[39] Because of these occurrences, residents of black Nashville consistently linked Greenwood Park and Greenwood Cemetery with Preston Taylor.

In 1913, the *Nashville Globe* honored Taylor for his twenty-five years as an apt entrepreneur, calling him the "friend of the struggling man. Not only that, but he is a friend to everybody." The paper also noted: "Greenwood Cemetery and Greenwood Park will forever stand as monuments to his credit. His life is wrapped up in these more than anything to which he has put his hand, and at the end of those twenty-five years there is no evidence of a slackening in his activities."

The *Nashville Globe* spoke for most black Nashvillians when its editor dubbed him a "tireless worker and his record made in this city as a business man and as a humanitarian stamp him as a man of the highest type."[40]

These words point again to the kindness, sacrifice, and selflessness reflected in the poem, "He's My Brother," composed by

---

[37] "Big Blaze," *Nashville Globe* (January 14, 1910): 1, 5.

[38] "Annual Picnic," *Nashville Globe* (July 22, 1910): 1. "Negro State Fair at Greenwood Park This Week," *Nashville Globe* (September 30, 1910): 1.

[39] "Sporting News," *Nashville Globe* (June 15, 1917): 8. "Prof. W. H. Mayo Visits Nashville," *Nashville Globe* (June 29, 1917): 5. "National Convention of Col. Church of Christ," *Nashville Globe* (August 23, 1918): 1.

[40] "Quarter of a Century's Progress," *Nashville Globe* (April 11, 1913): 1, 4.

Micah S. Combs, a white Disciple, who mentored Preston Taylor in the undertaking business. The fourth verse of Combs's poem reads:

> And when I see him faltering
> Beneath his heavy load,
> I'd go and help him carry it
> Along the rugged road.
>
> Though he may be no kin to me,
> And has a different mother,
> God is the Father of us both,
> Therefore he is my brother.[41]

Preston Taylor did not write the words, but he definitely lived them out. By forming Greenwood Cemetery and Greenwood Park, Taylor sought to create a resting place and a breathing place for African Americans in Middle Tennessee, his people, whom he collectively viewed as "my brother."

---

[41] Biographical File of Micah S. Combs, Jr., in DCHS.

Seven

"Riding the Goat"

Civic Organizations in Middle Tennessee

Defend the poor and fatherless: do justice to the afflicted and needy. —Psalm 82:3

Learn to do well; seek judgment, relieve the oppressed, judge the fatherless, plead for the widow. —Isaiah 1:17

Preston Taylor and the Prohibition Cause

In the summer of 1883, H. S. Berry, the talented preacher for the Gay Street Christian Church in Nashville, Tennessee, stirred up J. C. Graves, minister for a Christian Church in Paris, Kentucky, when the former said after preaching in Paris for a gospel meeting that the latter's flock was in a "lamentable condition." Graves took issue with this assessment and explained that many black congregants failed to attend Berry's meeting because they were "busy harvesting and short nights prevented many, who really wanted to hear Bro. Berry, from coming out." Berry's comments, charged Graves, placed him in a "bad light."[1]

Graves further defended his flock in Paris, stating that they had good elders and deacons. However, he expelled one deacon from office for "using ardent spirits." The fallen deacon confessed his shortcoming and vowed to "do better. Upon his promise they

---

[1] J. C. Graves, "Our Colored Brethren," *Christian Standard* 18 (September 15, 1883): 365.

restored him." But the deacon relapsed, and on August 30, 1883, church leaders met and "finally dismissed him; so I hope we are on the road to prosperity." Graves then explained why he supported the prohibitionist cause, declaring, "The reason we have so much whisky drinking in churches is the preachers are indirectly in favor of it. As Bro. Berry knows, it seems that they condemn it in one sense and sanction it in another—as Bro. Berry himself has greatly criticized, calling it a farce." Knowing that his Paris congregation was directly and negatively affected by one man's alcoholism, Graves concluded:

> Again, if because the Paris church has one man that drinks whisky, it puts the church in a lamentable condition, then every church among us is in a lamentable condition. Our church here is in lack of duty, like every other church, but we are now hard at work trying to put new life into it.[2]

But Berry denied the allegation that he opposed the prohibitionist movement. Fusing Latin phrases, Greek mythology, and scriptural references, Berry stated:

> So far as drinking whisky is concerned, we said nothing about it, though this was one of the things of which he complained. As to his temperance and prohibition declamations, if we were among the immortals on the golden heights of Olympas or with old Boreas, amid his white pavilions, we might be able to say a few things about them: as it is, they seem to us as the chasing of an ignis fatuus—and as to our being its friend, the ipse dixit was imbecile from birth, we taste, touch and handle it not.[3]

The Graves–Berry exchange illustrates that the prohibitionist movement did indeed infiltrate the Stone-Campbell movement and agitated African Americans in that fellowship. The abuse of alcohol disrupted Graves's congregation; thus, he fully supported the prohibitionist cause, whereas Berry seemed to hold a neutral position.

As early as 1855, residents of Tennessee injected prohibition into the gubernatorial election. Three decades later, prohibition

---

[2] Ibid.

[3] H. S. Berry, "Our Colored Brethren," *Christian Standard* 18 (October 6, 1883): 389. The Latin phrase, *ignis fatuus*, means something deceptive. The Latin phrase, *ipse dixit*, refers to a dogmatic, unproven statement. The words, "taste, touch and handle it not," are a reference to Colossians 2:21.

petitions numbered more than 18,000 names; however, this number fell significantly short of the 50,000 names required by the Tennessee legislature. white adherents of the Stone-Campbell movement held divergent views of prohibition. On the one hand, Silena Moore Holman, a white Christian from Fayetteville, Tennessee, emerged as a chief spokesperson for the Woman's Christian Temperance Union (WCTU), arguing that abstinence from alcohol would result in revival in the nation. She rebuked ministers who refused to join the prohibitionist cause, pleading with them to "give us the prohibition of the liquor traffic, give us the universal practice of abstinence among the followers of Jesus, and, with the blessing of God, we predict a speedy revival of religion in the church and a rapid extension of it over the world."[4]

On the other hand, David Lipscomb, a white preacher in the Stone-Campbell movement and the editor of the *Gospel Advocate*, disagreed with Holman's position and insisted that God could subdue the evils of alcohol without Christians' involvement in politics. With the exception of using alcohol for medical purposes, Lipscomb vigorously rejected drunkenness and recreational alcohol consumption. Still, he opposed the idea that "all ungodliness comes from intoxicating liquor, and if we destroy it, the world will become Christian."[5]

In 1885, when Preston Taylor settled in Nashville, he was one of 43,350 black residents living there.[6] In the same year, Tennessee lawmakers introduced a resolution urging African Americans to support the prohibitionist cause. Historian Ted Ownby has keenly observed that white Southerners were often frightened by the drinking behavior of black people.[7] African Americans themselves split over the temperance issue. For some black Tennesseans,

---

[4] *Gospel Advocate* XXVI (June 17, 1885): 378; cited in Paul E. Isaac, *Politics and Prohibition: Turbulent Decades in Tennessee, 1885–1920* (Knoxville: University of Tennessee Press, 1965), 26.

[5] Ibid., 26–27.

[6] Bobby L. Lovett, *The African-American History of Nashville, Tennessee, 1780–1930: Elites and Dilemmas* (Fayetteville, AR: University of Arkansas Press, 1999), 84.

[7] Ted Ownby, *Subduing Satan: Religion, Recreation, and Manhood in the Rural South, 1865–1920* (Chapel Hill, NC: University of North Carolina Press, 1990), 172. Commenting on the prohibitionist movement in Tennessee, author Elizabeth K. Goetsch observed that Levy's gin had made "more black rape fiends than all other agencies combined." Goetsch, *Wicked Nashville*, 84.

consuming alcohol was a personal decision and an expression of freedom. An African American farmer pledged: "I am going to vote for whisky. I am a member of the church. I goes for a Christian. I don't read and don't want to; it might change my mind. I love whisky and drinks it regular." Another black supporter of alcohol consumption called prohibition a "slave law"; and one more fussed, "I fought the rebels for my freedom, and I'll fight again before I will let prohibitionists take away my rights."[8]

However, the overwhelming majority of black Tennesseans supported the prohibitionist program. Influential nonresidents, such General Clinton B. Fisk and black statesman Frederick Douglass, appealed to African Americans in Tennessee to vote for the temperance amendment. African Americans collaborated and openly agitated for prohibition by rallying churches and the three black schools in Nashville—Fisk University, Roger Williams, and Tennessee Central College. Four thousand Nashvillians listened to North Carolina minister J. C. Price, who urged African Americans to fight liquor, which threatened to destroy their churches, homes, and opportunities for advancement.[9]

Preston Taylor was undoubtedly among the four thousand who heard the J. C. Price speech. Unlike David Lipscomb, who looked askance at Christians' involvement in politics, Taylor felt no misgivings about merging politics and religion. Scholar Bobby L. Lovett has shown that Taylor, a Christian Church minister—along with Methodist pastor John M. Gilmere and Baptist cleric William Haynes—helped to lead Nashville's Colored Prohibition Club. "They used music," asserts Lovett, "furnished by church choirs and local college glee clubs, ice creams, barbecue, and soda pop to attract the masses to the rallies."[10]

That observation provides insight into Taylor's theological, political, and sociological outlook. Not only did he freely mix religion and politics, he also willingly worked across denominational lines for the good of the broader black community. Additionally, for Taylor, recreational and festive events could be blended with church activities. Such a posture would eventually enrage leading conservative black members of the Stone-Campbell movement and

---

[8] Isaac, *Prohibition and Politics*, 37.
[9] Ibid., 36.
[10] Lovett, *The African-American History*, 87.

precipitate their withdrawal from the Gay Street Christian Church, resulting in the establishment of the Jackson Street Church of Christ in Nashville. Indeed, S. W. Womack, after coming under the influence of David Lipscomb and the *Gospel Advocate*, began railing against "innovations" practiced by black Disciples in the Gay Street Christian Church and the Lea Street Christian Church. After withdrawing from these congregations and launching the Jackson Street Church of Christ in Nashville, Womack affirmed, "We have no entertainments, no clubs, no ladies' aid societies; but we believe in meeting these obligations through the church, the God-given institution provided for all his work."[11]

'Riding the Goat Generally'

On August 17, 1865, African Americans in Nashville launched the first black Masonic Lodge, with thirty-seven members to "pool their resources and solicit money from the masses to start businesses and even cemeteries."[12] Two decades later, Preston Taylor relocated to Middle Tennessee, joined the black masons, and injected passion and enthusiasm into the organization. Like many upper-class and middle-class African Americans in Middle Tennessee, Taylor poured his heart and soul into the work of Freemasonry. At a spring 1908 meeting, black Masons in Nashville held a fundraiser for the benefit of several charitable institutions in the city. A *Nashville Globe* reported, "The auditorium was very generously donated for the occasion by the Odd Fellows' Hall Association at the head of which is that public-spirited citizen, Rev. Preston Taylor."[13] In short, Taylor was no private person or shy believer; he was an impassioned Christian leader who publicly and unabashedly stirred up the passions of others about issues that mattered to him.

Nine years later, Taylor delivered a keynote address to the Grand Lodge of Odd Fellows in Hopkinsville, Kentucky; and the same newspaper called him,

> a forceful and fluent speaker and is in great demand for fraternal meetings as he is a member of nearly all of the

---

[11] S. W. Womack, "Church News," *Gospel Advocate* 44 (April 10, 1902): 237. See also, Edward J. Robinson, *Show Us How You Do It: Marshall Keeble and the Rise of Black Churches of Christ in the United States, 1914–1968* (Tuscaloosa, AL: University of Alabama Press, 2008), 11–21.

[12] Lovett, *The African-American History*, 108.

[13] "Charity Entertainment," *Nashville Globe* (May 8, 1908): 6.

organizations and is well posted along the lines of grips, signs, passwords and riding the goat generally. It is said that he has ridden more kinds of goats than most any living man and knows exactly how to master the most rambunctious billy goat that ever lived.[14]

The phrase *riding the goat* suggests that candidates for initiation into fraternal groups were required to ride goats. This notion was widespread around the beginning of the twentieth century.[15] It is unclear whether Taylor literally rode a goat for his induction into Freemasonry, but what is clear is that the image merges with his personality of seriousness and determination. His indefatigable spirit compelled him to fight to the end.

Black involvement in Masonic work dates back to the Colonial Era, when Prince Hall, an abolitionist, launched the African Grand Lodge of North America to fight for liberty, education, and peace. As historian James Sidbury has insightfully observed, "George Washington may have been the father of the country and the most famous early American Mason, but Prince Hall was the father of African Freemasonry, leading a movement that expressed and fought for the interests of northern free black people."[16]

Like Prince Hall, Taylor experienced bondage, fought in the military, and yearned to help his people in a different era and in a different way. Taking his cue from James 1:27, "Pure religion and undefiled before God and the Father is this, to visit the fatherless and widows in their affliction, and to keep himself unspotted from the world," Taylor purchased property on the outskirts of Nashville in 1907 to establish a "Widows and Orphans Home for the Colored

---

[14] "Goes to Kentucky to Orate for Odd Fellows," *Nashville Globe* (July 13, 1917): 6.

[15] William D. Moore, *Riding the Goat: Secrecy, Masculinity, and Fraternal Jinks in the United States, 1845–1930* (New York: Oxford University Press, 2007).

[16] James Sidbury, *Becoming African in America: Race and Nation in the Early Black Atlantic* (New York: Oxford University Press, 2007), 74. Sidbury added: "From its inception, African Freemasonry was an organization of respectable and established black men, and Hall and his followers, like their white Masonic brothers in the craft, advocated positions on most political and religious issues that remained within the mainstream of elite opinion" (p. 75). See also Franklin and Higginbotham, *From Slavery to Freedom*, 107, 110–111, 116–117.

Masons."[17] In the mind of Preston Taylor, "pure" and primitive Christianity extended well beyond observing weekly communion and worshiping without musical instruments; it also involved helping the "widows in their affliction and train up the homeless and friendless orphans in the admonition of the Lord."[18]

A practical man, Taylor supervised the remodeling of the newly purchased home for orphans and widows.[19] In the spring of 1908, the Grand Lodge Convention changed venues to Nashville from Pulaski, Tennessee, the birthplace of the Ku Klux Klan, because of a recent lynching there.[20] When the meeting took place in mid-June, attendees saw the structure and were "inspired and delighted in the home for widows and orphans. The seeing of this valuable piece of land, it is believed, will inspire the members of the Order to rally and pay for the same before another year passes away."[21] Taylor gave a "strong, encouraging address before the Grand Lodge in the interest of the Home," and closed in "beautiful language" an invitation to return to Nashville.[22]

A visionary leader, Taylor participated in Grand Lodge meetings across Tennessee. He understood that he alone could not address the needs of the two thousand black orphans in the Volunteer State.[23] In the spring of 1907, he attended the Thirty-Seventh Annual Grand Communication of the Masonic Grand Lodge in Johnson City, Tennessee, to "wind up Orphan Home business."[24] A short time later, Taylor visited Knoxville, where he heard Dr. J. P. Crawford, the grand chancellor of Nashville, report that the organization had nearly $20,000 in finances and an enlarged membership of

---

[17] "Negro Masons of Tennessee," *Nashville Globe* (March 22, 1907): 8. See also "Masonic Widow and Orphan Home," *Nashville Globe* (February 22, 1907): 7. Masons touted the Christian virtues of brotherly love, relief, truth, fortitude, prudence, temperance, and justice. See *The Masonic Text-Book of Tennessee* (Nashville: Grand Lodge of Tennessee, 1866), 45–48. Jabez Richardson, *Richardson's Monitor of Free-Masonry; Being a Guide to the Ceremonies in All the Degrees* (New York: Lawrence Fitzgerald, 1860).

[18] "Negro Masons of Tennessee," *Nashville Globe* (March 22, 1907): 8.

[19] "City Items," *Nashville Globe* (April 3, 1908): 5.

[20] "The Grand Lodge Convenes Monday," *Nashville Globe* (June 12, 1908): 1.

[21] "Masons to Meet Here Again," *Nashville Globe* (June 19, 1908): 1.

[22] Ibid.

[23] Lovett, *The African-American History*, 108–109.

[24] "Masons Hold Annual Session in Johnson City," *Nashville Globe* (June 21, 1907): 7.

approximately five thousand.²⁵ The following year, Masons gathered in Murfreesboro, where Taylor gave a "powerful address ... reviewed the achievement of the societies and spoke many encouraging words to the delegates."²⁶

By 1917, African American Masons from Tennessee made their presence felt at national Grand Lodge conventions. Four months after the United States entered World War I, two hundred Tennessee delegates participated in the Grand Lodge National Convention in St. Louis, Missouri. There, the Volunteer Company No. 5 Drill Team, under the command of Brigadier-General Preston Taylor, won first place in the national drill contest. The *Nashville Globe* reported:

> Councils were held daily, and the four companies from Tennessee drilled from early morning until very late at night each day. Thursday morning when the competition drill was called for, these brave and fearless knights from sunny Tennessee came upon the parade grounds confident of victory. They were cheered by more than two hundred Tennesseans, who accompanied them.²⁷

The same paper added that Preston Taylor had finally "realized his dream by having the State of Tennessee to take her rightful place among them who are trying to accomplish things."²⁸ The military training, precise drilling, and rigid discipline Preston Taylor had acquired as a Union soldier during the Civil War stayed with him, and he consequently imparted those skills and virtues to fellow black Masons and others.

'A Busy Man All the Time'

Preston Taylor did ride many kinds of goats, and he wore many different hats. Dock A. Hart, managing editor of the *Nashville Globe*, succinctly captured how the preacher-mortician juggled multiple responsibilities: "Mr. Taylor is a busy man all the time and few men can conduct so many things at the same time as he and meet with

---

²⁵ "Eminently Successful," *Nashville Globe* (July 19, 1907): 1.
²⁶ "The Fortieth Annual Session," *Nashville Globe* (August 14, 1908): 1, 7.
²⁷ "Tennesseans at Supreme Lodge," *Nashville Globe* (August 31, 1917): 1, 4.
²⁸ Ibid.

like success. This fact is evidenced by the number of enterprises he is conducting now solely for the interest of the people."[29]

In addition to being a committed member and leader of the Grand Lodge (Knights of Pythias) Masons, Taylor served as a stockholder in the One Cent Savings Bank and Trust Company, established in 1904 to "encourage frugality" among African Americans. R. H. Boyd was the bank's president, Taylor chaired the board of directors, and Attorney J. C. Napier was the cashier.[30] Taylor also became president of the Tennessee Undertakers' Association, president of the Colored Citizen's Club, and a member of the National Negro Business League (NNBL).[31] Launched in 1900 by Booker T. Washington, the organization sought to create "cooperation" and to strengthen business practices among black entrepreneurs. Unlike W. E. B. Du Bois and others who promoted and prioritized the civil rights of African Americans in the formation of the Niagara Movement in 1905 and in the founding of the National Association for the Advancement of Colored People (NAACP) in 1909, Washington took an opposite stance and elevated economic development above civil rights. In his view, the success and prosperity of black people in business affairs would eventually solve racism in America. He expounded,

> Whether in the North or in the South, wherever I have seen a black man who was succeeding in his business, who was a taxpayer, and who possessed intelligence and high character, that individual was treated with the highest respect by the members of the white race. In proportion as we can multiply these examples, North and South, will our problem be solved.[32]

Preston Taylor and other black leaders in Middle Tennessee admired the "apostle of industrial education" and imbibed his principles, even as they agitated for civil rights in various ways.

---

[29] "New Funeral Car of Taylor & Co.," *Nashville Globe* (January 24, 1908): 8.

[30] Don H. Doyle, *Nashville in the New South, 1880–1930* (Knoxville, TN: University of Tennessee Press, 1985), 116. Lovett, *The African-American History*, 117–118. Gabriel A. Briggs, *The New Negro in the Old South* (New Brunswick, NJ: Rutgers University Press, 2015), 48.

[31] "National Negro Business League in Session," *Nashville Globe* (August 17, 1917): 1.

[32] Cited in Basil Matthews, *Booker T. Washington: Educator and Inter-Racial Interpreter* (London, UK: SCM Press LTD, 1949), 183–184.

Yet, Taylor had figured out the road to success long before Booker T. Washington launched the NNBL. Indeed, in his 1906 book, *The Negro in Business*, Washington highlighted Taylor as a model of achievement for aspiring black entrepreneurs.[33] In the mind of the Tuskegee educator, Taylor stood forth as "exhibit A" as to what hardworking black people can do. Even after the death of Washington in 1915, Taylor continued to support and attend the conferences of the NNBL. Three years later, the *Nashville Globe* announced that Taylor, Attorney R. L. Mayfield, Judge J. C. Napier, and other African American leaders in Nashville would be attending the NNBL in Atlantic City, New Jersey, the "playground of the rich and the leading summer resort in the United States."[34]

Because of his constant multitasking and his leading different ventures, Taylor undoubtedly suffered from extreme exhaustion. In the fall of 1907, he announced his plan to travel out West. When a *Globe* reporter inquired how long he would be gone, the evangelist replied:

> I do not know; I am going away to see if I can get some rest. It may be that I will get back in fifteen or twenty days; but I shall be back and will have had the rest needed, because it is my intention to give more time next year to fixing up Greenwood Park so that it will be the best in the city."[35]

A genuine perfectionist, Taylor desired to produce the "best" park in Middle Tennessee; and as a true workaholic, he went to rest with work on his mind (the refurbishing of Greenwood Park).

Before departing with his wife, Georgia Gordon Taylor, however, the women of the Lea Avenue Christian Church surprised him with a "beautiful four course luncheon." Mr. W. C. Wilkins gave closing remarks, and Ida Mallory (Preston Taylor's future and fourth wife) "sang a beautiful solo, 'We shall never forsake thee.'"[36]

Preston Taylor and the YMCA

Sir George Williams, a London retailer, organized the Young Men's Christian Association (YMCA) in 1844 to offer healthy activities

---

[33] Booker T. Washington, *The Negro in Business,* 100–101.

[34] "National Negro Business League," *Nashville Globe* (October 18, 1907): 1.

[35] "Rev. Preston Taylor on a Western Tour," *Nashville Globe* (October 18, 1907): 1.

[36] "Granted a Leave of Absence," *Nashville Globe* (October 18, 1907): 3.

for young men in major cities. Seven years later, the organization traversed the Atlantic Ocean and found a home in Boston, under the leadership of Thomas Valentine Sullivan, an American seaman and missionary. The institution eventually made its way to Nashville, Tennessee, in 1875, when white believers gathered at the Vine Street Christian Church.[37]

Because Jim Crow statutes barred African Americans from the organization, Preston Taylor, a lover of children, spearheaded an effort to form a YMCA for black youth in Nashville. The city's black paper announced, "The Negro is where he belongs but he needs to have such training as will make him manually capable, intellectually alert and moral straight. To give him just that training, there is no better equipped agency than the Y.M.C.A"[38] The announcement stirred black women across Nashville, who rolled up their sleeves and assembled fifty female captains, with each team consisting of twenty workers. The paper then pointed out, "As this account goes to press some of the leaders have their teams about complete and others are busy canvassing the field for twenty or more faithful workers."[39]

The women's hard work paid off, as three thousand (mostly black) residents braved inclement weather and packed the Ryman Auditorium to support the formation of a YMCA for Nashville's black youth. Mayor Robert Ewing gave his stamp of approval to the effort, stating,

> We need your co-operation and you need ours, and if the Y.M.C.A. is good for the white boys it is good for the Negro boys. We are your friends, but you must continue to show that the tremendous advance which you have made as a race was not by accident.

The mayor continued:

> We are going to help you, and we want every honest mother and father among you to do your part. You should get behind the movement and give it the right kind of support, moral

---
[37] C. Howard Hopkins, *History of the YMCA in North America* (New York: Associated Press, 1951).
[38] "The Negro Y.M.C.A.," *Nashville Globe* (February 2, 1917): 1.
[39] "Women Organize Y.M.C.A. Auxiliary," *Nashville Globe* (February 2, 1917): 1.

support as well as financial support. We cannot do for you what you can do for yourselves. This movement means the elevation of the colored race, and I congratulate you on the start which you have made. I stand ready to help you.[40]

J. H. Allison, another white official, told the predominantly black crowd, "God helps those who help themselves." He then acknowledged that the Fisk Jubilee Singers from Fisk University in Nashville brought national and global attention to the city. "The north and east," asserted Allison, "speak of Nashville as the home of Andrew Jackson and of Fisk University. It would be well for the Negro Y.M.C.A. to have such a reputation."[41]

Black Nashvillians gladly welcomed the verbal support from white dignitaries, but they were willing to help themselves. Still, the pledge of white support to a black movement in the Jim Crow South engendered hopeful sentiments. The *Nashville Globe* captured the mood:

> There has been an effort in which white and colored worked together for the cause dear to the hearts of the lovers of good citizenship and better manhood. It has been a mighty interesting history making event, and those who have had a hand in it, whether much or little, are sure to share proportionately in the good results which will follow.[42]

In the spring of 1917, the *Globe* reported that African Americans in Nashville had raised more than $20,000 toward the purchase of the Duncan Building to house the YMCA.[43] After securing the building, a clean-up committee, led by Taylor and others, announced a clean-up week after finding four hundred dirty windows, "beds to be cleaned, mattresses to be aired, walls and curtains swept, pictures taken down and dusted."[44]

Among the first events to be held at the newly restored building was a rally to send off Company G, a black regiment summoned for World War I duty. Preston Taylor urged all Nashvillians to the city-wide affair:

---

[40] "Three Thousand at Ryman Auditorium," *Nashville Globe* (February 16, 1917): 1.
[41] Ibid.
[42] "Latest Y.M.C.A. News," *Nashville Globe* (March 30, 1917): 2.
[43] "$20,140.88 Raised for Y.M.C.A.," *Nashville Globe* (April 6, 1917): 1.
[44] "The Call Is to All," *Nashville Globe* (April 20, 1917): 8.

Men, women and children are asked to come out and show their patriotism and loyalty in sending their boys to the front to fight for "Old Glory." All have been asked to come and shake hands with the boys and bid them Godspeed. The Committee of Management of the Y.M.C.A. has consented to turn over the spacious building for this occasion.[45]

Preston Taylor, Tennessee State University, and Patriotism

In the spring of 1910, African American leaders in Nashville organized to establish the first state-supported institution of higher education for black youth. William J. Hale, a high school principal, favored Chattanooga as a site for the new university, but Nashvillians Benjamin Carr and Henry A. Boyd pledged an additional $40,000 in bonds, and Nashville became the city of choice by the state board of education. An enthused Preston Taylor spearheaded this effort and arranged for the "daily reports of each canvasser" to be handed in to the "headquarters" of the Taylor and Company Funeral Home.[46] Taylor himself traversed the Volunteer State to raise funds for the proposed institution of higher learning. Indeed, his energy prompted the *Nashville Globe* to write,

> Dr. Taylor is one of the race's strongest leaders and has amassed a large fortune, and sole proprietor of one of the largest businesses in the Southland. Though more than sixty years of age, he is as active as a boy of sixteen. He has neither frowns nor gray hairs. Indeed, his is a happy, trustful nature seeing always the bright side of everything.[47]

Sixty-one-year-old Taylor was getting physically old, but he remained young at heart and cared deeply about the success of young African Americans.

After two years of strenuous toil and labor by Taylor, J. C. Napier, R. H. Boyd, and others, the dream of an institution of higher

---

[45] "Patriotic Demonstration for Co. G," *Nashville Globe* (August 3, 1917): 1.

[46] "Great Activity," *Nashville Globe* (March 18, 1910): 1. For the influential work of William Jasper Hale, see Tommie Morton-Young, *Nashville, Tennessee, Black America Series* (Charleston, SC: Arcadia Publishing, 2000), 57.

[47] "Educational," *Nashville Globe* (April 15, 1910): 1.

education for black youth became a reality in 1912 with the founding of Tennessee Agricultural and Industrial State Normal School for Negroes (now Tennessee State University). William J. Hale became the first president of the newly formed school. Walter S. Davis, with an earned doctorate from Cornell University, succeeded Hale to become the school's second president.[48]

During the World War I era, Taylor poured his energy and enthusiasm into young people beyond the YMCA, and he simultaneously displayed his deep patriotism. In short, he melded two passions: youth involvement and patriotism. He often visited Pearl High School, a historic, all-black school in Nashville. Organized by J. C. Napier in the 1880s in Trimble Bottom, it first became a high school in 1897 before relocating near Fisk University in 1916.[49] Taylor frequented this institution of learning and shared his experience as a Civil War soldier and his role in the famous Petersburg, Virginia, campaign. He then compared and "contrasted the destructive effects of [World War I] with the simpler methods with the War of Secession." He pointed to the "Service Flag" and explained, "Here we have a new flag, a Service Flag, which indicates that twenty-one young men as represented by the stars, have dedicated their lives to the service of their country." The *Nashville Globe*, when commenting on Taylor's speech, noted, "His appeal to the students to be Americans, to love the flag, to appreciate their citizenship, to remain loyal and patriotic, was a fitting perioration [*sic*] of an excellent address."[50]

Taylor returned to the same school the following month for a Service Flag ceremony. In his discourse, he explained the role of African American soldiers in the nation's past wars. He then "explained the color of the American flag, its history, and the reverence that we owe to it." After he asserted that the black man was "always loyal to his flag, and that the Negro is a success rather than a failure." Taylor then petitioned divine guidance for our soldier

---

[48] Morton-Young, *Nashville, Tennessee,* 57–65.

[49] "Pearl High School Notes," *Nashville Globe* (February 22, 1918): 7. For the historical significance of Pearl High School (now Martin Luther King Magnet School), see John Egerton, *Nashville: The Face of Two Centuries, 1780–1980* (Nashville, TN: Plus Media, 1979), 191; Morton-Young, *Nashville, Tennessee,* 48.

[50] "Pearl High School Notes," *Nashville Globe* (February 22, 1918): 7.

boys, after which, the student body gave the military veteran a "vociferous applause."[51]

Taylor did "ride many goats generally," as he immersed himself in various civic events to make life better for African Americans. He gladly participated in economic enterprises, Freemasonry, YMCA fundraisers, patriotic events, and high school activities, injecting passion and enthusiasm into every organization he served. In anticipation for an upcoming "Emancipation Celebration," the *Nashville Globe* noted: "Rev. Taylor took charge of the meeting and in his inimitable style soon injected life into the meeting."[52]

More than a charismatic leader, Taylor was deeply patriotic and longed to impart that spirit of loyalty to his young listeners. Indeed, he served in the military, sacrificed, and loved a country, even when that nation refused to love him and other African Americans in return. Nevertheless, Preston Taylor was a devoted soldier and a proud flag-waving American; yet, as the next chapter will show, he was above all a committed Christian who elevated the cross of Christ far above the American flag.

---

[51] "Flag Raising at Pearl High," *Nashville Globe* (March 15, 1918): 8.
[52] "Emancipation Celebration," *Nashville Globe* (January 3, 1908): 7.

Eight

Wrapped Up in the Lea Avenue Christian Church

Pastoral Ministry in Nashville

For what is our hope, or joy, or crown of rejoicing? Are not even ye in the presence of our Lord Jesus Christ at his coming? For ye are our glory and joy.
—1 Thessalonians 2:19-20

Trouble in the Church

In the summer of 1888, conflict erupted in the Gay Street Christian Church in Nashville, Tennessee. Organized in 1859, the congregation first met on 7th Avenue South, moved to Vine and Crawford Streets, and later became the Gay Street Christian Church. Preston Taylor succeeded H. S. Berry as pastor around 1886.[1] For the first two years of Taylor's tenure, African American Elders J. B. Williams, Thaddeus Cowan, and Thomas Pool approved having him as "teacher for the congregation." But the following year, church leaders at the Gay Street congregation wanted to dismiss Taylor, even though the women and young people wanted him to stay. The older members and deacons sided with the elders, who went to court to get a restraining order against Taylor to prevent him from

---

[1] Bobby L. Lovett, *The African-American History of Nashville, 1780–1920: Elites and Dilemmas* (Fayetteville: University of Arkansas Press, 1999), 28, 35–36.

"preaching or performing the functions of teacher in the church."[2] The trio of elders—Williams, Cowan, Pool—chose to oust Taylor on grounds of alleged sexual misconduct. Taylor then appointed four new elders—William Lawrence, Solomon Watkins, William Nichol, and Bedford Hughes—who wanted the preacher to stay. To help resolve the matter, the old elders invited white leaders to intervene in the dispute.

In addition, Nashville's Chancery Court (created in 1834 to handle minor legal cases) issued an injunction to prevent the new elders—Lawrence, Watkins, Nichol, and Hughes (whom Preston Taylor ordained)—"from acting in that capacity." White church leaders in Nashville—Reuben Lindsay Cave, R. M. Giddens, A. D. Wharton, John G. Houston, and David Lipscomb—intervened, investigated the "controversy," and gave the following report. First, black shepherds at the Gay Street Christian Church—Williams, Cowan, and Pool—accused Taylor of "immoral conduct," but Lipscomb and his white cohorts found insufficient evidence to "establish the charge."[3] Second, the Cave panel explained that "as the elders have the spiritual welfare of the church in their hands, they have a scriptural right to say who shall be their minister or preacher." The Cave committee ruled that Williams, Cowan, and Pool were the "lawful officers" of the Gay Street Christian Church, and that the congregants acted in an "unreasonable and unscriptural" manner by taking the "government of the church out of the hands of their scripturally constituted rulers." In short, Gay Street adherents wanted the shepherds terminated only when they refused to extend Taylor's tenure as local preacher.[4]

The Cave jury then ruled that the "election" of the quartet of elders appointed by Taylor was "illegal" and "unscriptural." Cave and his colleagues concluded,

> We recommend that the existing board of officers remain unchanged, for the present, until such time as your arbitrators, and as a means of promoting peace and harmony in the meantime and in view of the fact that the deacons appear to be unmixed with the troubles, we further

---

[2] R. Lin Cave, "Church Trouble Decided," *Gospel Advocate* 30 (July 4, 1888): 2.
[3] Ibid.
[4] Ibid.

recommend that the elders request the deacons to direct the services of the church.[5]

David Lipscomb used the conflict at the Gay Street Church of Christ to outline his views on church government and to explain why he, Cave, and the other mediators made their decision. First, the "Holy Spirit," affirmed Lipscomb, "has made elders the rulers and teachers of the church of God." Citing Acts 20:28, 1 Peter 5:1, 1 Timothy 5:17, 1 Timothy 3:2, Titus 1:9, and Hebrews 13:17, Lipscomb averred: "These Scriptures plainly teach that God has committed under himself the teaching and rule of the congregation to the elders." Second, the *Gospel Advocate* editor cited 1 Timothy 2:12, 1 Corinthians 14:34, and 1 Peter 5:5 to argue,

> [S]electing a teacher by a popular vote takes this right of teaching and ruling out of the hands of the elders, and places it in the hands of women, the youths and the inexperienced of the congregation. In this way the whole government of the church as ordained by God is subverted.[6]

Lipscomb vehemently opposed "turning out and putting in elders, by popular vote, without a careful selecting, and consideration of the qualifications as laid down by the Holy Spirit." On one hand, Lipscomb maintained that elders held in their hands ecclesial governing authority; on the other hand, he cautioned overseers "not to seek to rule in a dictatorial, arbitrary manner. But they are to rule by submissive devotion of themselves to the will of God and a kindly, earnest effort to advance the good of every member."[7]

But Preston Taylor rejected the Cave–Lipscomb verdict and subsequently moved in an independent direction, launching the Taylor Funeral Company in 1888 and the Lea Avenue Christian Church a few years later. Historian Hap Lyda has noted that Rufus Conrad, a churchman from Louisville, Kentucky, assisted Taylor in organizing the Spruce Street Christian Church. In 1892, Taylor purchased a lot for $1,250 on Lea Avenue, deeded it to the church, erected a tent, and held worship services and rallies for funds. Two years later, the congregation erected a forty-foot square building and

---

[5] Ibid.
[6] Ibid.
[7] Ibid.

dedicated it as the Lea Avenue Christian Church.[8] More importantly, the quarrel at the Gay Street Christian Church provides a glimpse into the theological, ecclesiastical, racial, and cultural tension swirling inside the Stone-Campbell movement in the late nineteenth century. Theologically, whereas Lipscomb deemed the elders "over" the preacher in ecclesial affairs, Taylor clearly believed that the minister held equal, if not greater, authority than the shepherds. From enslavement to emancipation, the black preacher emerged as the premier leader in both the African American church and community.

Furthermore, that R. Lin Cave, R. M. Giddens, A. D. Wharton, John G. Houston, and David Lipscomb—all white arbitrators—presided over dissension at an all-black congregation attests that white paternalism pervaded race relations in the Stone-Campbell movement. Knowing that Anglo leaders controlled the papers and resources, many African American leaders expressed divergent opinions about submitting to white dominance. On the one hand, S. R. Cassius, a former enslaved person who emerged as a leader in the Stone-Campbell movement in Oklahoma, in 1889 chided white leaders who viewed black men as a "set of numbskulls." He believed that African Americans were just as good morally and intellectually as white people.[9] On the other hand, Alexander Campbell, an ex-slave and former associate of Preston Taylor, welcomed white beneficence and intervention, announcing, "Dear white brethren, some of the loyal colored brethren have the zeal, the whole truth, and the courage to do the right thing, and you white brethren who are loyal have the zeal, the whole truth, the courage, and the money."[10]

Preston Taylor's break from the Gay Street Christian Church demonstrates that he would have aligned with Cassius's posture. Yet, Taylor obviously maintained cordial ties with R. Lin Cave, who, after the Gay Street controversy, became president of Transylvania College. When Taylor's third wife, Georgia Gordon Taylor, died in 1913, Cave, then pastor of the Woodland Street Presbyterian Church in Nashville,

---

[8] Hap Lyda, "A History of Black Christian Churches (Disciples of Christ) in the United States through 1899" (PhD diss., Vanderbilt University, 1972), 94.

[9] Edward J. Robinson, *To Save My Race from Abuse: The Life of Samuel Robert Cassius* (Tuscaloosa: University of Alabama Press, 2007). Robinson, *To Lift up My Race.*

[10] Alexander Campbell, "Our Colored Brethren," *Gospel Advocate* 51 (1909): 1523. See also Robinson, *Show Us How You Do It,* 28.

attended and shared words of comfort.[11] After the conflict at the Gay Street Christian Church, Taylor organized the Lea Avenue Christian Church in Nashville.

'That Man of the People'

Preston Taylor practiced open fellowship. Because he was involved in so many organizations and clubs, he spoke in and supported denominational churches. After installing officers for the Benevolent Treasury No. 5, he gave an "excellent address" at the Fifteenth Avenue Baptist Church.[12] Taylor preached in Baptist and Methodist churches and their pastors, in turn, preached to his congregation. In the winter of 1908, he informed *Nashville Globe* readers that Bishop Evans Tyree would preach at the Lea Avenue Christian Church, adding that he was "always delighted to have him speak at his church."[13] Later that summer, Taylor invited Tyree to give the Emancipation Day celebration address at Greenwood Park.[14] The annual celebration, coinciding with the dedication of the recently renovated Greenwood Park, prompted the *Globe* to call Taylor, "that man of the people."

On Easter Sunday of 1918, Taylor preached at the Spruce Street Baptist Church in Nashville. The following month, he preached for Reverend D. T. Burch at the Braden Memorial Methodist Episcopal Church.[15] Even the Gay Street Christian Church, from which Taylor had broken away, invited their former pastor to return and preach to help retire their debt of $800.[16]

Taylor clearly aligned with the theology of the mature Alexander Campbell of the *Millennial Harbinger* instead of the Alexander

---

[11] Reuben Lindsay Cave (1845–1924) was born in Virginia, fought for the Confederate Army, and ministered to the First Christian Church and the Vine Street Christian Church in Nashville, Tennessee, before becoming president at Transylvania University from 1897 to 1899. Reuben Lindsay Cave File (DCHS) in Bethany, West Virginia. For Cave's eulogistic remarks about Georgia Gordon-Taylor, see "Jubilee Singer Gone," *Nashville Globe* (June 13, 1913): 4.

[12] "Benevolent Treasury No. 5," *Nashville Globe* (January 17, 1908): 6.

[13] "Bishop Tyree at Lea Avenue Christian Church," *Nashville Globe* (March 13, 1908): 2.

[14] "To Be Delivered by Bishop Tyree," *Nashville Globe* (July 31, 1908): 1.

[15] "Braden Memorial Church," *Nashville Globe* (March 15, 1918): 4. "Two Annual Celebrations," *Nashville Globe* (April 26, 1918): 3.

[16] "Grand Rally and All Day Services at Gay Street Christian Church Sunday, May 26th, 1918," *Nashville Globe* (May 24, 1918): 3.

Campbell of the *Christian Baptist*. The younger Campbell—writing, preaching, and teaching from 1823 to 1830—espoused a combative spirit and a legalistic perspective; the Campbell of the *Millennial Harbinger* from 1830 until his death in 1886, was more open, more mature, and more cordial toward other religious groups. In his 1837, *Lunenburg Letter*, he publicly declared that he believed there were "Christians among the sects." Twelve years later, he became president of the American Christian Missionary Society, the very organization he had denounced during his *Christian Baptist* days.[17] Like the Campbell of the *Millennial Harbinger*, Preston Taylor had no qualms about using extra-congregational groups and clubs to accomplish the work of God.

The Lea Avenue Christian Church also played host to numerous entertainment and festive activities. In the spring of 1907, the congregation awarded necklaces to adolescents Lillian Cooper and Ethel M. Ferrell for "selling large numbers of tickets for the entertainment given recently." Ms. Cooper actually won the prize but, like a doting and impartial father, Taylor "gave the little Ferrell girl a little necklace just like the one the other little girl won. This was done because little Ethel sold such a large number, and also to encourage her." The two clubs, the Reds and the Blues, raised $65.60 to help retire the church's debt.[18] Such activities—deemed unscriptural by some African Americans in the Stone-Campbell movement—propelled S. W. Womack, Alexander Campbell, and Marshall Keeble out of the Christian Church. The trio helped form the nucleus for what became the Jackson Street Church of Christ in Middle Tennessee.[19]

In the summer of 1907, the Lea Avenue congregation honored Taylor for his thirty-eight years in the Christian ministry. When addressing his congregants during the occasion, the pastor spoke on the subject, "Mindful," and stressed "what a powerful mind God had equipped man with to remember the things that are godly—things that are pleasing to God; to remember to do the deeds of charity that we have performed during our lives." In a "masterly effort" and

---

[17] Richard T. Hughes, *Reviving the Ancient Faith: The Story of Churches of Christ* (Grand Rapids, MI: Eerdmans, 2006/1996).

[18] "Presentation at Lea Avenue Church," *Nashville Globe* (June 28, 1907): 4.

[19] Edward J. Robinson, *Show Us How You Do It: Marshall Keeble and the Rise of Black Churches of Christ in the United States, 1914–1968* (Tuscaloosa, AL: University of Alabama Press, 2008).

before an attentive audience, the black evangelist said that he "had tried and would always endeavor to impress upon his congregation the importance of being mindful of our Creator."[20]

During the Thanksgiving holiday, Preston Taylor's congregation invited black Nashvillians to attend its "Thanksgiving Dinner and Concert." For a ten-cent admission fee, the public could hear musical entertainment by the "Sniggles family, see a drill performance by the Lea Avenue Guards. Companies A. and B. and enjoy a hot dinner during the day and a cold lunch at night."[21] In the spring of 1908, the Lea Avenue Christian Church hosted a "May Festival and Bazaar," a three-day affair with an "Old Folks Concert" on Monday; a "May Pole Drill and crowning of the May Queen on Tuesday; and a Tom Thumb Wedding and Military Drill by Companies A. and B. The event was open to the public with a ten cents admission fee."[22]

The festivals and fundraisers held by the Lea Avenue Christian Church congregation paid off. In the fall of 1908, the congregation held its dedicatory services free of monetary debt. Organized in 1888 by Preston Taylor with assistance from Rufus Conrad of Louisville, Kentucky, the Lea Avenue flock began with one hundred members. W. H. Dickerson delivered the keynote address and noted, "There is not a church in history whose congregation has accomplished so much in such a short while." Patient toil and financial prudence enabled Taylor and his followers to erase $4,000 worth of debt, while erecting a building, buying furniture, and renovating "from basement to auditorium for this occasion."

"For beauty," the *Nashville Globe* exclaimed, "there is not another church in the city that can surpass it." The local paper heaped further praise on Preston Taylor:

> The congregation of Lea Avenue should be ever grateful to their pastor, Elder Preston Taylor, who has been with them for the past twenty years, for it has been through his most strenuous efforts that the congregation has been so successful. Elder Taylor, who is always ready to assist or do something for the enjoyment of others generally succeeds in whatever he undertakes.

---

[20] "Thirty-Eight Anniversary," *Nashville Globe* (August 2, 1907): 1.
[21] "A Thanksgiving Dinner and Concert," *Nashville Globe* (November 22, 1907): 2.
[22] "May Festival and Bazaar," *Nashville Globe* (May 15, 1908): 6.

Ever the idealist, optimist, and perfectionist, Taylor was committed to offering to God a debt-free facility. The *Globe* editor then explained, "The reason the church has not been dedicated before this is, the pastor and congregation did not want to give it to the Lord in debt. So it was dedicated free of all debt."[23]

Free and clear of monetary indebtedness, the Lea Avenue Christian Church pressed forward in charitable works and opened its doors to various denominations, professionals, and fundraising events. On October 19, 1908, Taylor and his flock hosted a benefit for a charity ward at the Wilson Infirmary and succeeded in "every way." Bishop Evans Tyree and Judge J. C. Napier were among those who gave encouraging remarks. Women in attendance donated towels, pillow cases, and sheets; and while several men and preachers contributed financial gifts of one dollar each, Preston Taylor gave twenty-five dollars.[24] As the year closed, the pastor preached an "excellent sermon," titled, "Where Are We Going When We Die?" to a "good congregation."[25]

Less than a decade later, the Lea Avenue Christian Church again honored Taylor for forty-eight years in the preaching ministry. "Forty eight years is quite a long time," a *Globe* reporter noted, "but Elder Taylor has been in the ministry that long and looks good for a great many years more." During the occasion, the youth department presented him with "beautiful bouquets of flowers," and senior members became emotional when reflecting on the "early days of the church." Taylor responded with "one of his clever characteristic talks." He then reviewed the history of the Lea Avenue congregation and "praised his members for their unswerving loyalty to the church and their pastor," adding that "his whole mind and soul was wrapped up in Lea Avenue Christian Church and its splendid membership."[26]

Preston Taylor worked in a lot of professions and endeavors—the undertaking business, the railroad industry, as cemetery and park operator, in Freemasonry—but his primary preoccupation

---

[23] "Lea Ave. Church Dedicated," *Nashville Globe* (September 11, 1908): 1.

[24] "Concert at Lea Avenue Church," *Nashville Globe* (October 23, 1908): 3.

[25] "City Items," *Nashville Globe* (December 4, 1908): 6.

[26] "Elder Preston Taylor Forty-Eight Years in the Ministry—Anniversary Celebration," *Nashville Globe* (August 3, 1917).

was pastoral ministry. His work and labor as a preacher fueled all his other endeavors.

Preston Taylor and Foreign Missions

Yet Taylor was more than a local pastor. He reached out and supported Christian missionary work in foreign nations. In the winter of 1913, Taylor and the Lea Avenue Christian Church hosted R. J. Dye, a white missionary to Monrovia, Liberia (Africa), for fifteen years. Dye shared his experiences in and "conditions of Africa," and Taylor and his congregants pledged $500 to support Africa missions.[27] Dye had worked alongside African American missionary Jacob Kenoly who, while working as a hotel clerk in Conyers, Georgia, came under the influence of a white Christian named D. A. Brindle. The latter told Kenoly about the "Christian Church and the simple New Testament plea" and directed him to J. B. Lehman and the Southern Christian Institute in Edwards, Mississippi. Kenoly enrolled there, studied there three years, and worked eventually as a missionary to Monrovia, Liberia. In 1905, he and his wife, Ruth, organized a boarding school. The couple engendered much evangelistic and educational success until Jacob's tragic drowning in 1911.[28]

In addition to supporting missionary activity in Africa, the Lea Avenue Christian Church pledged monetary assistance to mission efforts in China. The *Tennessean,* a local paper controlled by white Nashvillians, reported,

> The congregation of Lea Avenue Christian church, of which Rev. Preston Taylor is pastor, pledged itself to raise five hundred dollars towards the establishment of a missionary hospital at Chamdo, China, at a mass meeting held at the church Wednesday night, following addresses by a number of missionary workers of the Christian church now in the city.[29]

---

[27] "Dr. Dye at Lea Avenue," *Nashville Globe* (March 7, 1913): 1.
[28] C. C. Smith, *The Life and Work of Jacob Kenoly* (Cincinnati: Methodist Book Concern, 1912), 13, 18. See also, C. C. Smith, "Africa," *The Gospel Plea* (November 11, 1911): 12. "Jacob Kenoly," *Christian Standard* (July 22, 1911): 39.
[29] "Local Negroes to Aid the Heathen Chinese," *Tennessean* (January 30, 1913): 12.

The Two Wives of Preston Taylor in Nashville, Tennessee

Georgia Gordon Taylor

After Taylor relocated from Kentucky to Tennessee, he married Georgia Gordon Taylor in 1890. Born in 1855 in Nashville to enslaved parents Mercy Duke and George Gordon, Georgia in her early teens enrolled at Fisk University, where she sang and traveled with the renowned Fisk Jubilee Singers. Organized by George L. White, the nine African American singers (seven of whom were former slaves) began traveling across the United States and Europe to raise funds for the fledgling school. While on tour, an immature Georgia fell in love with another Jubilee singer, but he was married man, Frederick Loudin. The inappropriate relationship never blossomed.[30]

After returning and settling in her hometown, she met and married a newcomer to the city and the new preacher for the Gay Street Christian Church. The date of their marriage is uncertain, but their only child, Preston G. Taylor, died at seven months. Even though the tragic loss devastated the young couple, Georgia continued to play an active and crucial role in her husband's pastoral ministry. Mrs. Taylor continued to use her musical talent to stir up audiences across Middle Tennessee. During the Christmas season of 1907, she reunited with Mrs. George W. Moore (also known as Ella Shepherd, an original member of the Fisk Jubilee Singers) and others to sing "psalms, hymns, and spiritual songs."[31] Taylor displayed her husband's liberal spirit when she donated $53.65 to the Day Home in Nashville to assist underprivileged children. The *Nashville Globe* took notice of her generosity, writing:

> Words of praise of the lovely spirited woman who conceived this entertainment and carried it out so successfully for the benefit of the Home at a time of its greatest need cannot be too many or too high. There is no greater joy on earth to bring comfort and sunshine to an unfortunate little one. This is what Mrs. Taylor has done.[32]

---

[30] Andrew Ward, *Dark Midnight When I Rise: The Story of the Jubilee Singers Who Introduced the World to the Music of Black America* (New York: Farrar, Straus and Giroux, 2000), 337.

[31] "Cantata at Fisk During the Holidays," *Nashville Globe* (December 13, 1907): 1.

[32] "Mrs. Preston Taylor Gives $53.65 to Day Home," *Nashville Globe* (December 27, 1907): 3.

The black women of Nashville observed her leadership skills and chose her to chair the women's auxiliary for the Colored State Fair of Tennessee.[33] She and her female cohorts wanted to showcase the artistry and craftworks of black people in their community. In her speech before a large crowd on the Fair's opening day, Georgia Taylor said,

> The women of our organization have felt for a long time the need of some effort of this character to exhibit the skill and handiwork of our men, the deft and artistic tastes of our women, and even the aptness with which our children take to anything pertaining to manual training.

She reserved her highest compliments for the faithful women, who "worked zealously, refusing to be discouraged. As a result we present to you the exhibit below, hoping you can at least realize something of the effort we have put forth to procure even this exhibit."[34]

When she was not organizing efforts for the annual Fair, Georgia Taylor consistently accompanied her husband to charity events, dinner parties, and, of course, church services. Such constant activity, like her workaholic husband's, without question fatigued and exhausted her body, soul, and mind. Indeed, the *Nashville Globe* noted that after the 1908 State Fair, Sister Taylor departed Nashville for Cincinnati, Ohio, to "spend several weeks in that city." Two years later, the local media announced that Mrs. Taylor spent nine weeks in Florida to "recuperate her health," adding that she looked the "very picture of health, and [the] visit has added ten years of youth to her appearance and spirits."[35]

Notwithstanding her extended respites, Mrs. Taylor returned to the hustle and bustle of life in Middle Tennessee; by 1913, her health had seriously declined. Just before the annual Easter egg hunt at Greenwood Park, Preston Taylor told a *Globe* reporter that the

---

[33] "The Colored Fair Association," *Nashville Globe* (January 31, 1908): 3.

[34] "First Annual Exhibition," *Nashville Globe* (September 18, 1908): 1.

[35] "City Items," *Nashville Globe* (September 25, 1908): 6. For charity and community work to which Mrs. Georgia Gordon-Taylor contributed, see "The Algonquins Give Charity Masque Party," *Nashville Globe* (March 13, 1908): 4. "The Needs of DAP Home," *Nashville Globe* (May 22, 1908): 2. "Thanking the Public for Their Patronage," *Nashville Globe* (September 25, 1908): 8. For Mrs. Taylor's nine-week visit to Florida, see "City Items," *Nashville Globe* (April 8, 1910): 5.

prizes would be "much larger" than ever before; however, in a tone of sorrow, he confessed that he "has been somewhat handicapped in his arrangements, as Mrs. Taylor, who has worked so constantly with him from year to year, is still ill, unable to do much work along this line."[36] Two months after that interview, Georgia Gordon Taylor, Preston Taylor's third wife, passed away.

The front page of the *Nashville Globe* displayed a beautiful picture of Georgia Gordon and noted,

> [She had] suffered for several months, and the end was not a surprise to those who had some knowledge of the condition and in the fact she herself realized several months ago that it was only a question of time with her. She was most patient in her affliction, always exhibiting a spirit of cheerfulness.

Over a three-day period, a "stream of people [went] to and fro to take a last look at this good and grand woman." The *Globe* commended members of the Nashville community who came to comfort her bereaved husband, noting, "Every undertaker in the city, both black and white, rushed to the side of Mr. Taylor and offered to him every aid in their power. It is admirable indeed the way in which his colleagues rallied to his rescue."[37]

Ella Shepherd, a fellow Fisk Jubilee Singer with Georgia Taylor, said that her colleague's "quiet, unassuming, cheerful spirit never failed us in all of our struggles, and she did what she could in every way to pass on what she had enjoyed to others, and her work will continue to bear fruit in the years to come."

One of Preston Taylor's closest ministerial friends in the Christian Church, W. H. Dickerson, offered these comforting words: "We shall not know the worth and influence of our dear sister who has gone to her home on high, in this life, but we shall know it better when the mists have rolled away."[38]

Ida Mallory Taylor

Close friends of Georgia Taylor reported that she actually died of a broken heart because of the loss of her infant child and because her

---

[36] "Easter Egg Hunt at Greenwood Park," *Nashville Globe* (April 4, 1913): 5.
[37] "Another Jubilee Singer Gone," *Nashville Globe* (June 13, 1913): 1.
[38] Ibid., 4.

husband fell in love with a younger woman.[39] The younger woman was most likely Ida Mallory. When the Lea Avenue Christian Church granted Preston Taylor a leave of absence in 1907, the congregation gave him a surprise send off. A fair-skinned, tall, slender young lady with a melodious voice, Ida sang a "beautiful solo."[40] Did Georgia Taylor's extended absences from Nashville to improve her health lead to her husband's affair with Ida? We are not sure, yet we can properly surmise that Ida's face, figure, and pretty voice indelibly stamped her preacher; he was smitten.

In 1916, Preston and Ida tied the knot. Like his third wife, Ida served beside her renowned husband as a hostess at tea parties, formal dinner parties, and fundraising events.[41] The following year, she traveled with her husband to the Midwest "in the interest of the Christian Church." Preston Taylor delivered a keynote address before a predominantly white audience, and his "talented wife had the charge of the song services at these meetings which is enough to assure that the singing was of high order." The couple garnered "much social attention by leaders of society" in St. Louis and Kansas City and an even warmer welcome when they returned home.[42]

In short, although little is known about Taylor's first wife, Ellen (or Ella), it is known that three of his wives—Anna, Georgia, and Ida—were all members of the Christian Church and exercised leadership roles among African American women in their chosen fellowship. Anna gave speeches before conventions to encourage women and young people in her faith tradition. Georgia sang and helped organize Easter egg hunts at Greenwood Park and chaired the women's organization for the Tennessee State Colored Fair. Ida served as a Sunday school teacher and used her melodious voice at funerals, dinner parties, and other special occasions. Extant information shows that at least two of Preston Taylor's children died in infancy. Did these tragedies contribute to the dissolution of at least two of his marriages? Or did workaholism doom them? Or did he simply succumb to fleshly desires? Perhaps we will never know the exact answers to those questions.

---

[39] Emma W. Bragg, *Scrapbook: Some Family Reminiscences of a Native Nashville Septuagenarian* (n.p., 1985), 7. See also Ward, *Dark Midnight*, 395-396.

[40] "Granted a Leave of Absence," *Nashville Globe* (October 18, 1907): 3.

[41] "Madam Harris Honored," *Nashville Globe* (January 19, 1917): 5. "Mr. C. A. Dickson Returns Home," *Nashville Globe* (January 26, 1917): 5.

[42] "Home Again," *Nashville Globe* (November 9, 1917): 7.

Other contemporary and noteworthy black leaders and preachers in African American church history have been ensnared in extramarital affairs and sordid relationships. Indeed, the four marriages of Preston Taylor resemble the four marriages of Henry McNeil Turner, a renowned bishop in the African Methodist Episcopal (AME) Church. When Turner's third wife, Harriet Wayman, passed away in 1907, he married twenty-seven-year-old Laura Pearl Lemon, who was divorced from an AME minister. Because Bishop Turner was forty-six years older than Lemon, this union ignited a storm of controversy in his chosen fellowship. [43] When Preston Taylor's third wife, Georgia, died in 1913, he was sixty-four years old; in the same year, his fourth wife, Ida, was thirty-five. There is no known extant evidence as to whether members of the Lea Avenue Christian Church or black residents in the broader Nashville community openly complained or protested the preacher's fourth marriage. Yet, we do know that he was an accomplished man with great flaws.

Notwithstanding his moral failings, Taylor continued to preach and serve as the spiritual leader for the Lea Avenue Christian Church. Indeed, four years after Georgia's death, he pushed his way through sorrow, found new love, and launched the National Christian Missionary Convention (NCMC) in Nashville, becoming its first president. A man with an iron will and an indefatigable spirit, Taylor demonstrated that he refused to allow his imperfections and disappointments to stop him from achieving greater things.

---

[43] Stephen Ward Angell has shown that Bishop Turner's first wife, Eliza Ann Peach, died in 1889; his second wife, Martha DeWitt, passed away in the summer of 1893; and his third wife, Harriet Wayman, widow of Bishop Wayman, died in 1907. See Steven Ward Angell, *Henry McNeal Turner and African-American Religion in the South* (Knoxville, TN: University of Tennessee Press, 1992), 24–25, 240–245.

Part 4

Preston Taylor and the National Christian Missionary Convention, 1917-1931

Nine

'Onward Christian Soldiers'

The National Christian Missionary Convention, 1917-1919

Go ye therefore, and teach all nations, baptizing them in the name of the Father, and of the Son, and of the Holy Ghost.
—Matthew 28:19

Onward, Christian soldiers,
Marching as to war,
With the cross of Jesus,
Going on before.   —Sabine Gould

The first two decades of the twentieth century comprised the "worst of times" and the "best of times" for African Americans. On one hand, the Springfield Race Riot of 1908, the production of the anti-black movie *Birth of a Nation*, and the rebirth of the Ku Klux Klan in Stone Mountain, Georgia in 1915 all converged to make this period the worst of times and reminded black Americans that their white counterparts refused to see them as equals. Racial oppression across the South, coupled with the lure of economic opportunities in the North, drove half-a-million black Southerners out of their homeland in search of promised lands in Northern and Western communities in the so-called Great Migration.

On the other hand, the creation of the first black fraternity (Alpha Phi Alpha in 1906) and the first black sorority (Alpha Kappa Alpha in 1908), the founding of the National Association for the

Advancement of Colored People (NAACP) in 1909, the forming of the National Urban League in 1911, and the establishing of the Center for the Study of Negro Life in 1915 by Carter G. Woodson all combined to make this period the best of times, as black people, although oppressed, determined to help themselves socially, morally, intellectually, and economically.[1]

In this complex and tumultuous milieu, Preston Taylor poured his talent, time, and toil into the spiritual uplift of his fellow African Americans by organizing the National Christian Missionary Convention (NCMC). Five months after the United States entered World War I, Taylor and the Lea Avenue Christian Church in Nashville hosted the First General Convention.[2] The host preacher called the convention to order on Wednesday morning, September 5, 1917, and was at "himself in making the introductory speech. He welcomed the delegates in a quiet pleasant speech." The organizer then introduced Elder H. L. Herod, a delegate from Indianapolis, Indiana, who assured his racially mixed audience that the purpose of Convention was not to "destroy anything or anybody; but that better understanding and harmonious action is the aim."[3]

In the afternoon session, Elder R. E. Pearson, a minister of a Christian Church in Paducah, Kentucky, and corresponding secretary of the NCMC, addressed the topic, "Christian Leadership." Citing examples from secular and biblical history, Pearson delineated principles of true Christian leadership. First, he pointed to Booker T. Washington, who exhibited his sincerity in believing that industrial education was a right for the masses. Pearson explained: "There is

---

[1] Franklin and Higginbotham, *From Slavery to Freedom*, 286, 327-379. I have borrowed the phrase, "the best of times" and "the worst of times" from Charles Dickens (1812–1870), whose novel, *A Tale of Two Cities*, described conditions in eighteenth-century London and Paris. Dickens added: "it was the age of wisdom, it was the age of foolishness, it was the epoch of belief, it was the epoch of incredulity, it was the season of Light, it was the season Darkness, it was the spring of hope, it was the winter of despair, we had everything before us, we had nothing before us, we were all going to Heaven, we were all going direct the other way." See Charles Dickens, *A Tale of Two Cities* (South Naples, FL: Trident Press International, 1859/2000), 1.

[2] "Negro Disciples of Church of Christ," *Nashville Banner* (September 7, 1917): 16.

[3] *Report of the First General Convention of the Christian Church Colored in the United States September 5-9, 1917* (Nashville, Tennessee), 3; located in the DCHS Archives, Bethany, WV.

a secret about a real Leader. He first must know that he is right and must be sincere." The Tuskegee educator, Pearson added, touted his program of industrial education,

> line upon line and precept upon precept. So, finally his sincere appeals based upon RIGHT began to break down prejudicial bars and enhanced the doctrine of the brotherhood of man; and, converted men and women of both races forthwith put their dollars and thousands of them at Booker's proposal.[4]

Pearson then upheld white Kentucky statesman Henry Clay as a model of diplomacy, another important virtue for Christian leaders. He confessed,

> I have read bits of history of Mr. Clay and his work. I've heard men talk who met the congressman in person and heard him speak often, against strong opposition, on the vital political issues of his day. And the prevailing opinion is that if any one thing more than [any] other made Clay the successful Leader he was in world affairs, it was his great store of Diplomacy.[5]

In Pearson's view, Christian leaders, like Clay, should possess the "grace" of diplomacy.[6]

Pearson further presented the biblical character Joshua as a model of a godly leader:

> When speaking of military tactics and generals who have won signal victories for their country and worthy causes, one would be derelict of duty if special mention is not made of Joshua, the son of Nun. If I were to name what seems to me his most prominent virtue; I would at once say courage.[7]

---

[4] Ibid., 11

[5] Henry Clay (1777–1852), known as the great compromiser and the great pacificator, helped to keep together a divided nation on three different occasions: the Missouri controversy of 1819-1820, the nullification crisis of 1832, and the compromise of 1850. See, James L. Abrahams, *Men of Secession and the Civil War, 1859-1861* (Wilmington, DE: Scholarly Resources, 2000).

[6] *Report of the First General Convention*, 11.

[7] Ibid.

Pearson concluded his address by commending white Christians for their support of African American evangelists in foreign and domestic missions; by chiding Anglo Disciples for not including black people in leadership roles to "speak our sentiment"; and by challenging both races to "use this conference to the perfecting of a national body with sane Christian Leadership that we can the better understand the white Christian people's plans and purposes and be the better prepared to work with them both to will and to do His good pleasure."[8]

After Pearson's speech, white delegates gave talks and led discussions. J. H. Lehman, a white educator from Edwards, Mississippi, urged his listeners to think and look beyond themselves, asserting that "people should think so much of self, in terms of self; that men should not think of their own race." He then added that he had "always had in mind the development of a race as a policy in school work. That purely intellectual education will not save a race."

Anna Atwater, a white Christian from Indiana and president of the National Christian Woman's Board, reported that her organization was the "best friend" of African Americans. She then acknowledged that her association was a "big work" and that the work in behalf of black people was "only one item of it." She further indicated that she "expected the future to show greater work done on part of colored and white people for the advancement of the Kingdom."[9]

On the next day, Preston Taylor gave a strong address on "The Status and Outlook of the Colored Brotherhood," advocated for greater unity between white and black churches, emphasized higher educational standards, and forecast a brighter future for African American Disciples. His speech is instructive on several levels. First, he demonstrated his understanding of his chosen fellowship's historical ties to Barton W. Stone and the Cane Ridge Revivals in Kentucky. Enslaved Africans came under the influence of white leaders such as Stone, Samuel Rogers, John T. Johnston, and John Allen Gano and "could not be disobedient to the heavenly vision more than other human beings."[10]

---

[8] Ibid., 12.
[9] Ibid., 2.
[10] Ibid., 21.

Second, while applauding black Disciples alignment with the Stone-Campbell movement, he at the same time lamented the "smallness" of African American Disciples congregations:

> We have no newspapers of national import, no general organizations or meetings. Our churches are free to have fellowship in giving to the national work of the church. But even here, there is maintained no propaganda of education and inspiration through special workers, with the exception of a Bible school secretary recently put out by the American Christian Missionary Society, and the work done under the auspices of the Christian Woman's Board of Missions.[11]

Taylor then attributed the paucity of black adherents to Disciples of Christ to the pervasive influence of black Baptists and Methodists, declaring,

> It is true today that nine colored persons out of ten belong in some sense either to the Baptist or to the Methodist Churches. These institutions were early in the field of colored evangelization. Moreover, the methods used were such as appealed strongly to the untrained, emotional nature of the black man.

In Taylor's view, the emotionalism of Baptist and Methodist tenets and worship services triumphed over the rationalism of Stone-Campbell teachings:

> At all events, we are not far removed from the day when a colored Campbellite was considered the extreme of audacious perversity and blasphemy—a man with a head or book religion or no religion at all. Even now in winning enlightened colored persons to the cause of New Testament Christianity, one is called upon to break down family tradition and prejudice.[12]

Here, Taylor echoed a sentiment expressed by S. R. Cassius and Marshall Keeble, fellow African American leaders in the Stone-Campbell movement. In 1922, the former fussed: "I have had to win my way through religious prejudice in my own race and race

---
[11] Ibid., 22.
[12] Ibid., 23.

prejudice among the brethren of my own faith." A few decades later, Keeble lamented that he was hated by the white man because of his race and by the black man because of his religion, commenting, "The Negro didn't like my religion, and the white man didn't like the color of my skin. So I had to rely on God."[13]

Notwithstanding the religious prejudices of his black neighbors, Taylor specifically indicted white Disciples for the paucity of African Americans among Disciples of Christ. "The attitude of our white brotherhood on the race question accounts largely for our smallness. Without intentional wrong or neglect, the relation of the white to the colored brotherhood has been little more than trifling." He then added that the black man was

> simply let alone, separated by an ever increasing and corroding class spirit which denied [management] so much needed. Indeed in some striking instances, the Disciples of Christ have set the pace in heartless, unnecessary and silly racial discrimination. They have not found it difficult to strain at the gnat of human brotherhood or sectarian irregularity which [sic] they swallowed the camel of racial bigotry or un-Christian policy.[14]

Dr. Lawrence A. Q. Burnley has cogently argued that Taylor's speech critiqued white supremacist views in the Stone-Campbell movement and compelled white adherents to expand

> white restorationist biblical interpretation and theology asserting that Christian unity and living out the biblical mandate to restore the primitive church must include racial equality in every social, economic, and political sphere. In a real sense, Taylor implies a rejection of white Disciples theology due to the wide gap between the

---

[13] For the Cassius quote, see Edward J. Robinson (ed.), *To Lift up My Race: The Essential Writings of Samuel Robert Cassius* (Knoxville, TN: The University of Tennessee Press, 2008), xxi. For the Keeble quote, see Willie Cato, *His Hand and His Heart: The Wit and Wisdom of Marshall Keeble* (Winona, MS: J. C. Choate Publications, 1990), 10. See also Edward J. Robinson (ed.), *A Godsend to His People: The Essential Writings and Speeches of Marshall Keeble* (Knoxville, TN: University of Tennessee Press, 2008), xvi.

[14] *Report of the First General Convention*, 23.

rhetoric of Christian unity and the love of Christ and their dehumanizing treatment of Blacks.

Nevertheless, Taylor's speech ended with a tone of optimism, as he asserted,

> I am ready to reaffirm my faith in the simple religion of Christ and in the Disciples of Christ as the most faithful exponents of Him. They represent the faith of my fathers for more than a hundred years. I believe the Disciples of Christ have the message of salvation for my people, as for all people, for all time, world without end. Amen.[15]

Later in the convention, W. H. Dickerson, a preacher and delegate from Crofton, Kentucky, delivered a "most excellent address" titled, "The Negro Disciples and the Apostolic Program." He challenged his listeners in three areas. First, he urged fellow Disciples to let their light shine and endeavor to be true Christians "not in WORDS, but in DEEDS." "There is no power in wealth, no power in words to save men," declared Dickerson, "but there is no power equal to that of a life which reflects that of the Christ." Second, he challenged his audience to give more liberally, arguing, "One of the great sins of God's people has been, and is now, the failure to make liberal offerings and sacrifices to the Lord and for his cause."[16]

Third, after highlighting the church as "God's great organized body and power in the earth to make it worthy of a temporary dwelling place for men," Dickerson pled with fellow preachers to lead morally upright lives. He then cited Moses Lard, an influential white preacher in the Stone-Campbell movement who emphasized that Christian ministers should live pure lives, preach the truth, and be competent to preach, noting, "He who has these three qualifications owes it to Christ and the human race to preach: He who lacks them, should never attempt it."[17]

Dr. W. A. Scott, a delegate and educator from Texas, spoke on the subject, "The Importance of Co-operation in the Work of the Kingdom." After asking the cause of so few laborers in the God's

---

[15] Lawrence A. Q. Burnley, *The Cost of Unity: African-American Agency and Education in the Christian Church, 1865-1914* (Macon, GA: Mercer University Press, 2008), 248. *Report of the First General Convention*, 14.
[16] *Report of the First General Convention*, 14.
[17] Ibid., 15.

Kingdom, Scott answered, "ALL DIVINE and GOD Ordained WORK REQUIRES SELF-DENIAL! SACRIFICE! HUMILITY! Those who seek worldly HONOR, GLORY, Pleasure, the sweets of this life care not for the Life to come." From Scott's perspective, worldly Christians "mind the things of this world and consequently success in the highest and truest sense will never be achieved!" Another key point of Scott's lecture was unity. He asserted,

> If they were and are One, if Christ, God and the Holy Spirit are one, and if the apostles were and are on in Faith and Practice, and if we are followers of God and Christ, and the Apostles, as Dear Children, the Logical conclusion is WE MUST BE ONE in thought and action, faith and practice to inherit Eternal Life.[18]

On Friday morning, J. C. Napier, an influential Nashville attorney and close associate of Preston Taylor, attended a session and made a "nice speech, expressing interest in Rev. Taylor, of Nashville, Tenn., and the Christian Church." The delegates then voted to reconvene the NCMC in Nashville in 1919. On Saturday, Taylor generously supplied a special trolley car and gave delegates a tour of "many interesting parts of the city, and to the penitentiary where a guide showed them the various departments of the prison." The delegates to the convention gathered and worshiped at the Lea Avenue Christian Church on Sunday morning and afternoon, and then adjourned.[19]

In the summer of 1918, the NCMC returned to Nashville. During an informal report to the advisory committee, Taylor informed his audience that "no tangible work" had been accomplished since the year before because of the obstacles of World War I. Indeed, out of the 2,290,525 black men who registered for the war, only 367,000 were called into action. The convention's president then "offered a touching prayer in regards to the great evangelistic problems before the race."[20]

---

[18] Ibid. 18–19.

[19] Ibid., 8–9.

[20] *Report of the Second National Convention of Colored Christian Churches, September 9–15, 1918* (Nashville, Tennessee), 2, located in the DCHS Archives, Bethany, WV. For the number of African American men who were involved in World War I, see Franklin and Higginbotham, *From Slavery to Freedom*, 329.

On Wednesday morning of the convention, Elder Harry G. Smith, state evangelist for Texas, who had recently returned as a missionary to Africa, gave a stirring address, advancing the notion that "we as a race should aim at the best and not be contented with less." Smith stressed the importance of proper and positive thinking. Moving in the right direction required thinking the right thoughts. "We must realize that thought is power," he insisted, "and teach the principles of right thinking. Thought is the force with which we build and shape the whole future of our lives, whether for good or ill. Men are usually what they think they are."[21]

Smith then pointed to the courage and heroism of African Americans in the nation's historic wars. From the Revolutionary War to the Spanish-American War, he explained, black soldiers had "played their part by the side of their brothers in white, in removing the foreign fetter from the limbs of the nation." In the Civil War, approximately 180,000 African American men fought alongside white Union troops to "maintain the national union." He then referenced Fort Wagner, Milliken's Bend, and Petersburg as being some of the "greatest battles" of the Civil War.[22] (Union Army veteran Preston Taylor likely smiled when hearing these words.)

Smith further observed that the Buffalo Soldiers, comprising the Ninth and Tenth Calvary and the Twenty-Fourth Infantry, fought with Theodore Roosevelt and the "Rough Riders" and "made victory possible in the Spanish-American War. I pause here to ask this question, is not this bit of history an evidence of physical prowess, patriotism and courage." He appropriated these historical accounts to prod his listeners at the NCMC to step out with bold faith and "do the greater work for the kingdom."[23]

Smith accentuated the noteworthy accomplishments of Booker T. Washington, Jacob Kenoly, and Alexander Cross. Washington, refusing to allow the "hills of difficulties" to thwart his path, bequeathed the great Tuskegee, "which has been a blessing to the world." Smith lauded the courageous efforts of Alexander Cross and Jacob Kenoly, both of whom died while working as missionaries in Liberia, Africa. Cross, a former slave from Kentucky, "fought and fell" in Africa in 1854 after contracting "immigrant's fever." Kenoly, an

---

[21] *Report of the Second National Convention*, 14.
[22] Ibid., 15.
[23] Ibid.

African American from Georgia, converted to the Stone-Campbell movement and went to teach the restoration plea in Liberia. After yielding impressive educational and evangelistic success, Kenoly tragically died during a fishing incident in Liberia. Smith explained that even though Kenoly had "gone to rest," it was his desire that members of his race should carry on that work. Smith believed that black people were more effective in reaching out to their own race. "There is no living man," he affirmed, "who can go so close to the heart or get so deep into the confidence of an African as a member of his own race. This is true no matter what may be said to the contrary."[24]

In his concluding remarks, Smith reminded fellow believers that African Americans had "made good in the army in every great war of the country, and in the treasury department of the nations, and he has given a missionary hero to the world." Therefore, he urged his listeners to follow Jacob Kenoly into Liberia, Africa, as there are others who are "willing to lay their lives on the altar for Africa."[25]

After Smith's presentation, James H. Thomas, an instructor for the Christian Church at Martinsville, Virginia, gave a "thoughtful speech" titled: "Making Democracy Safe for the World." Basing his understanding of democracy on Galatians 3:28, Thomas insisted that "democracy must be all-inclusive." Knowing that black Southerners had their civil rights strategically swept away by Jim Crow laws, he added that democracy must

> cover all men beneath her protecting wings. If any are to be denied the blessed boon of her loving care, they must be excluded as individuals and never as groups. She must neither be bedazzled by the purple and fine linen of kings nor feel contempt for hodden [sic] gray of the horny-handed peasant."[26]

After Thomas delivered his address, NCMC leaders introduced Mrs. Ida V. Jarvis, principal donor to the newly established Jarvis Christian Institute in Hawkins, Texas. Later that afternoon, she

---

[24] David Edwin Harrell, Jr., *Quest for a Christian America: The Disciples of Christ and the American Society to 1866, Volume 1* (Nashville, TN: Disciples of Christ Historical Society, 1966), 95–96. See also Lester G. McAllister and William E. Tucker, *Journey in Faith: A History of the Christian Church (Disciples of Christ)* (St. Louis, MO: Bethany Press, 1975), 258. *Report of the Second National Convention.*, 15.

[25] Ibid., 16.

[26] Ibid., 17.

addressed the subject, "The Why of Her Love for Negroes."[27] The content of her speech is not known to be extant, but her generous donation of land for the education of African Americans in East Texas is a testament to her concern for humanity and her interest in democracy.

On Thursday morning (September 11), Taylor introduced African American benefactors, Mr. and Mrs. J. C. Napier, who both made "remarks of friendly feeling." Mr. Napier bestowed verbal bouquets on the NCMC.[28] The following morning, Elder R. E. Pearson, a churchman from Paducah, Kentucky, spoke on the subject of "Church Extension," in which he urged his fellow Disciples to build "attractive and serviceable Church houses." The unity plea of the Christian Church was itself appealing, yet there must be a more concerted effort to erect appealing facilities, he noted, proclaiming, "The religious position we have in the world and the great plea we are making for union and unity are within themselves unique." He then advised fellow black clergymen to apply for funds to build a "better house" through the Church Extension Board, under the auspices of G. W. Muckley of Kansas City, Missouri. Pearson shared his own congregation's experience with the organization in Paducah, where they worshiped in an unattractive, dilapidated building until they received monetary support from the Church Extension Board. Because of the generosity of "Muckley's Board," Pearson testified that a "house was built; membership increased, and the church bettered in every way," adding, "And there is no color line with the Board. They do business for Christ and humanity."[29] In an era of rigid racial separation, Disciple leaders endeavored to reach across racial barriers to expand the borders of the Lord's kingdom.

On Friday night, R. H. Davis, a church leader from Ohio, expounded on the topic of democracy, emphasizing, "Making the World Safe for Democracy." In the context of World War I, he upbraided those who relied on politicians and political policies to establish peace and security in the world. Biblical teachings, he said, would create safety in the world. He added,

> To make the world safe for democracy, there must be a new system of education and this new system must be granted

---
[27] Ibid., 4.
[28] Ibid., 5.
[29] Ibid., 20.

to all peoples and races and the Bible must be the central force in it; for no individual, race or nation will be safe for the principles of democracy until that individual race or nation knows God.[30]

W. H. Dickerson, a "high church man" from Lockland, Ohio—using an analogy from the story of the Good Samaritan who came to the aid of a wounded traveler—challenged believers at the NCMC to

> get off its worldly beast and pour in oil and wine to heal the terrible wounds that sin, through greed, has made. And not only pour in oil and wine to heal the wound and find refuge for the wounded, but the church is challenged to find the highwaymen, and by some righteous means stop them from repeating their inhuman treatment of mankind.[31]

In the mind of Dickerson and his fellow Disciples, the oil and wine represented the gospel of Jesus Christ, "the power of God unto salvation."

The year 1919 marked the occurrence of what author and activist James Weldon Johnson labeled the "Red Summer," a period of intense racial violence sweeping across the United States against African Americans, who returned from serving in World War I and as black people chose to fight back. Race riots erupted in Elaine, Arkansas, Knoxville, Tennessee, Longview, Texas, Washington, D.C., and Omaha, Nebraska. The most deadly occurred in Chicago, Illinois, where fifteen white people and twenty-three black people were killed; five hundred people suffered injuries over a two-week period; and thousands of families, mostly African Americans, were left homeless.[32] In this racially hostile environment, the Third NCMC convened again in Nashville on September 2–7, 1919.

Participants in the Third NCMC felt the sting of the racial strife. Indeed, on Wednesday night of the program, Mrs. M. J. Stearns, a delegate from Indianapolis, argued that white and black Christians held the solution to America's race problem, stating that African American "Christians could do much to stay race friction, by holding

---

[30] Ibid., 22.
[31] Ibid., 21.
[32] Rayford W. Logan and Irving S. Cohen, *The American Negro: Old World Background and New World Experience* (New York: Houghton Mifflin, 1967/1970), 173. See also Franklin and Higginbotham, *From Slavery to Freedom*, 358–364.

down members of the race; while white Christians can do much to the same end by holding down members of that race." The good news of Jesus, she stressed, contained power to eliminate racial strife and division. "There is nothing that will save the world," she affirmed, "save the message of Jesus Christ; that we should pray, pray, and pray until we have overcome every decisive influence."[33]

Later during the conference, Mrs. William Alphin, a delegate from Kansas City, Missouri, delivered a rousing address titled, "The Present Emergency and Its Challenge to the Womanhood of the Church." Mrs. Alphin specifically challenged women in the Disciples of Christ to rise up and "save the day." After acknowledging that God had used Germany and World War I to "challenge the world's Christianity," she saw the church in a state of "emergency" because of the racial violence inflicted on African Americans, who were being "burned at the stake." On one hand, the presence and participation of black soldiers in World War I prompted daily papers, religious journals, churches, and even President Woodrow Wilson to condemn lynching. Mrs. Alphin asked, "What caused this great change?" Then she answered: "God had spoken to mankind through the war. You are all my children and are thrown back on the same plane."[34]

On the other hand, she challenged her audience to work for greater racial harmony. She especially pled with Christian women to teach their children God's will for racial peace, asserting:

> The womanhood of the church can save the day. "The hand that rocks the cradle rules the world." This an old adage, but true. The babe in the mother's arms is as plastic as the potter's clay. She can mold and shape the life of that child in its most perceptive period to be what she wills it to be. Shall we so teach our children that they may grow up to respect each other as brothers and sisters of another race? The challenge to the womanhood of the church is threefold. The home life, educational and religious life of the young people must be cared for.

Race hatred, according to Mrs. Alphin, originated in chattel enslavement in the Colonial period, and biased parents perpetuated

---

[33] *Report of the Third National Convention; Second National C. W. B. M. Convention, September 2-7, 1919* (Nashville, Tennessee), 5, located in the DCHS Archives, Bethany, WV.

[34] Ibid., 18.

it. Innocent children, she added, "grow up to love and stay and stand by each other." Who causes them to separate as adults on the basis of race? She answered, "The mothers of these boys." Thus, she concluded: "The challenge is to the womanhood of the church: Will we be large enough at heart to say we are sisters, and as sisters in this emergency when race riots are common to get together and consider the things that tore us down?"[35]

Sister Alphin's speech clearly shows that while African American women were indeed concerned about the spiritual advancement of their faith tradition, they were equally concerned about the civil rights of their fathers, husbands, sons, and daughters being protected.

In essence, the first three NCMCs took place under the hegemony of Preston Taylor and the Lea Avenue Christian Church in Nashville, and they occurred in the immediate context of World War I, an environment rife with racial animus, national chaos, and global rumblings. In this backdrop, Taylor stepped forward and organized the NCMC to provide spiritual strength and stability to black and white members of the Stone-Campbell movement. Yet, as the various speeches and discussions over the three-year period reveal, Taylor and his cohorts clearly understood that racial tension and social tension swirling around the United States directly impacted their lives. Therefore, African Americans Disciples of Christ were forced to see themselves as soldiers on two fronts—contending earnestly for "the faith which was once delivered unto the saints" and fighting to protect the lives of black folk from racial oppression.

---

[35] Ibid., 19.

Ten

'March on to Victory'

The National Christian Missionary Convention, 1920–1931

We're marching to Zion,
Beautiful, beautiful Zion.
We're marching upward to Zion,
The beautiful city of God.—Isaac Watts

Sing a song full of the faith that the dark past has
    taught us
Sing a song full of the hope that the present has
    brought us
Facing the rising sun of our new day begun
Let us march on till victory is won.
            —J. Rosamond Johnson and James Weldon Johnson

Historians of the American experience have generally described the 1920s as the New Decade. The rise of a new economy (Henry Ford's assembly line), a new religion (fundamentalism), a new woman and morality (the flappers), a new music (the Jazz Age), a new "Negro" (Alaine Locke), a new literature (the Agrarians), and new heroes (George Herman "Babe" Ruth) all combined to make the second decade of the twentieth century the so-called New Era. As historian Jeanne Boydston has noted, the 1920s "promised new freedom to women and youth. It held out an alluring vision of material pleasures—a life devoted to leisure and consumption—to all Americans."[1]

Yet, "all Americans" did not include black Americans. In this milieu of economic and technological advancement, racial friction continued to ripple across the United States. In the spring of 1921, Dick Rowland, a nineteen-year-old black man in Tulsa, Oklahoma, allegedly physically assaulted a seventeen-year-old white woman named Sarah Page. Local authorities arrested Rowland and then spread rumors that he would be lynched. When black men came to jail to protect Rowland, a fight ensued and gunfire was exchanged, igniting the Tulsa Race Massacre. The race riot ended with thirty-nine dead people, twenty-six blacks and thirteen whites. Future historian and scholar John Hope Franklin, born and reared in Rentiesville, Oklahoma, recalled that the racial upheaval in Tulsa kept his family divided for more than four years.[2]

Alarmed and distraught over the reports about Tulsa, Preston Taylor, Rosa Brown Grubbs, and J. B. Lehman launched a nationwide "Emergency Campaign," not to address racial violence specifically but to focus on energizing and mobilizing Disciples of Christ. Mrs. Grubbs lamented that forty percent of Disciples congregations had "no pastors at all," adding, "This being true the majority of our churches do not 'meet upon the first day of the week to show His death and suffering until He comes.' As a result, the spiritual effect is bad and there is not the growth there should be." When asked, "What is the crying need of our churches?" Grubbs replied, "Prepared ministers." The goal of the "Emergency Campaign" was to raise $20,000 to establish a Christian college, to organize a Christian Church in Washington, D.C., and to aid in foreign missions.[3]

---

[1] Jeanne Boydston et al., *Making a Nation: The United States and Its People, Combined Edition* (Upper Saddle River, NJ: Prentice Hall, 2002), 679. See also, John Hope Franklin and Evelyn Brooks Higginbotham, *From Slavery to Freedom: A History of African Americans* (9th ed.) (New York: McGraw-Hill, 1947/2011), 368–416.

[2] Ibid. Tim Madigan has called the destruction of the "Black Wall Street" in Tulsa, Oklahoma, "Like Judgment Day." Tim Madigan, *The Burning: Massacre, Destruction, and the Tulsa Race Riot of 1921* (New York: Thomas Dunne Books, 2001), 1–6. John Hope Franklin, *Mirror to America: The Autobiography of John Hope Franklin* (New York: Farrar, Straus and Giroux, 2005), 4, 15–16. See also, Scott Ellsworth, *Death in a Promised Land: The Tulsa Race Riot of 1921* (Baton Rouge, LA: Louisiana State University Press, 1982).

[3] *Emergency Campaign Program for Emergency Campaign Special Rally*, July 31, 1921, 4, 6, 10.

The Fifth National Convention of Christian Churches was held at the Jarvis Christian Institute, a newly established college for African Americans in Hawkins, Texas. One of the focuses of this conference was Sunday school work in local churches. P. H. Moss, a field secretary for Bible schools, voiced his view that the modern Bible school was inadequate:

> The all too short half hour on Sunday, the untrained teacher, coming poorly equipped and prepared for even that half hour have all tended to reduce the efficiency and effectiveness of our present system of religious instruction, and for this reason there has been an increasing desire to introduce a workable plan of week-day religious education.

Moss presented a chart illustrating his points, and he explained the number of black Bible schools, adding that the "daily vacation school" goes a long ways in meeting the needs of the "great unoccupied fields."[4]

Evangelism and "soul-winning" were other principal topics to surface during the fifth convention. Elder William Alphin, a church leader from Kansas, urged all preachers to "hold a meeting for someone, organizing classes for piercing and inspiring." Harry G. Smith, a delegate from Texas, reiterated Brother Alphin's point, declaring, "The church has but one great program and that is redeeming man from the curse of sin." He further emphasized the need to reach across racial boundaries:

> Beyond any doubt we must work together, we must work as one great body in Christ whether we are white or black, brown, read or yellow if we are children of God we are obedient to his command and will. We are going to do our best as brethren forgetting color or previous condition we will put our hand in His and march on to victory as His children.[5]

W. P. Martin, a delegate from Tennessee, similarly gave a keynote address, titled: "Church Erection and Extension." Martin highlighted the need that, once black Disciples are baptized,

---

[4] *Minutes of the Fifth National Convention of Christian Churches in America, August 23-28, 1921* (Jarvis Christian Institute, Hawkins, Texas), 7, 9.

[5] Ibid., 40.

they must be housed—that is, provided a church building. We must realize, elaborated Martin, the "great need of more church buildings and better buildings, to glorify our Lord and Master. Open air evangelization and leaving groups of newly baptized here and there, without shelter is in my judgment, a great mistake." In his view, a "religious body that builds much, prospers much. A religious body that does not build, dies." For Smith, the evangelist's work was pivotal; and for Martin, the "Church Builder contributes to the permanency of the work of the evangelist." Using a military illustration, Martin added, "The builder of the bulwark holds the territory taken by the soldiers of the Cross."[6]

In 1922, the NCMC assembled in Indianapolis, Indiana, focused on strengthening Bible school programs across the Christian Church brotherhood. The president supported this emphasis and acknowledged,

> [The] transforming power of the Word of God on the lives of those who are brought intelligently in touch with it. From our own experiences and our observations of other lives we are convinced that the only life that is truly successful, the only one that is really worth living is that of a Christian.

Preston Taylor, although an affluent man, urged his listeners to grasp after the true and lasting wealth, not the false and transitory wealth. "We must see our task clearly," he proclaimed, "see ourselves as workers together with God and behold mankind around us reaching out eagerly to grasp the gems of life and ours the privilege of pointing them to the true ones and helping to destroy that which is false."

He especially challenged the crowd in Indianapolis to reach for a higher "Standard of Efficiency" in the Bible school ministry. While exhorting Bible school teachers to strive for greater effectiveness, he chided incompetent and irresponsible instructors, lamenting,

> I have seen teachers coming in ten and fifteen minutes late and still worse, I have seen teachers sitting before their classes who had made no preparation whatever for the teaching of the lesson and the short and precious moments filled with golden opportunities for impressing and changing a life were wasted.

---

[6] Ibid., 44–45.

Taylor again encouraged his audience by pointing to the eternal rewards God has promised God's faithful servants.[7]

In 1924, the Eighth National Christian Missionary Convention convened in Chicago, the so-called Promised Land for many African Americans during the First Great Migration.[8] In the Windy City, seventy-five-year-old Preston Taylor stepped forward and delivered the principal address. Knowing that he was in his declining years, Taylor displayed an other-worldly perspective. "Every one builds his own house that he lives in," he preached, "not only here but hereafter. The only thing we carry out of this world with us is our work."

Inspired by the mission and mandate of Jesus who urged his follower to "continue the work as I have begun," Taylor asked his audience, "have you sent any one to heaven? Have you any one on the road that leads to the city whose builder and maker is God? What is your work? What has it amounted to?" He then implored his listeners: "May I ask that you place your treasures in the hands of God and frequently visit where you have deposited and there to meet the Heavenly Friend that brings greater riches than the powers of the world can bestow."[9]

Taylor used the podium to bestow commendations on fellow black Disciples. First, he applauded the national workers—Mrs. Rosa Grubbs, Professor P. H. Moss, Miss Deesy L. Blackburn, and Elder William Alphin—for "measuring up to the task before them. Like the early pioneers, they do not find their pathway strewn with flowers or rosebuds, nor palace cars. They find on the other hand the valley and the mountain, their appointments and disappointments; all of these things they have met and overcome." He then cheered impoverished Disciples for "bringing and laying upon the altar hundreds of dollars, and in many instances reaching a thousand." He further exhibited a demeanor of black pride, stating,

> Instead of being ashamed of the race that we are identified with, it is an honor to be numbered with such an earnest set of people who in these last few years have built their own

---

[7] *Minutes of the Sixth National Convention of Christian Churches in America, August 21–27, 1922* (Indianapolis, Indiana): 13–15.

[8] Rayford W. Logan and Irving S. Cohen, *The American Negro: Old World Background and New World Experience* (New York: Houghton Mifflin, 1967/1970), 170–171.

[9] *Eighth National Convention of the Churches of Christ of the United States August 26–31, 1924* in (Chicago, Illinois), 24–26.

homes, churches to worship their God in school houses to educate their children in and giving to every worthy cause that demands their support.[10]

Additionally, in the spirit of Booker T. Washington, Taylor used his allotted time to urge African Americans to work for

> [A] clean community to draw from. If their morals are of a high type, the condition of the home have their family altars in them, daily bible readings, constant prayers and their offerings going up as a memorial before God. You may expect a church from such a community entering into the work with greater zeal and more endurance.[11]

Taylor was not only concerned for the Lea Avenue Christian Church in Middle Tennessee, he also had a heart for his chosen fellowship nationally.

In 1925, the National Christian Missionary Convention met in Cincinnati, Ohio. W. H. Dickerson, a delegate from Lockland, Ohio, gave an important address on "The Officers of the Church, How Chosen and Ordained." According to Dickerson, church officers—evangelists, elders, and deacons—must have the "vision, see the Man of Macedonia, and ears to hear the cry, 'come over and help us.' And behind all this, there must be the WILL to go over and help."[12] His brief remarks capture the core qualities of Preston Taylor's leadership skills: He was a visionary leader with a determined will and drive to succeed, to make things happen.

Mrs. William Alphin, a delegate from Kansas, urged her audience to collaborate with "white sisters in helping to preach the gospel to every creature" and to select "right leadership," a leadership that will "build up and not tear down." She then lamented that other denominations, including Baptists and Methodists, offered more colleges to black youth than did the Disciples of Christ:

> Brothers and sisters, have you not groaned within yourselves when you have noted the number of colleges among the Methodists, Baptists, Congregationalists? If you

---

[10] Ibid., 26-28.
[11] Ibid., 29.
[12] *Minutes of the Ninth Annual National Christian Missionary Convention of the Churches of Christ of the United States, August 24–30, 1925* (Cincinnati, Ohio), 20.

have not, I have. Are we not compelled to send our boys and girls to other church schools for their college work? I just want to lay this burden on your heart that we may do our part for one college and a Bible College in each school.[13]

Two years later, delegates to the National Christian Missionary Convention came together in Louisville, Kentucky. Preston Taylor again gave the main speech, which is not known to be available in full length. Yet, in substance he exhorted his audience to be doers of the word and to fulfill their commitments. After visiting churches in North Carolina, Illinois, Kentucky, and Ohio, he stated, "We must stop making resolutions and stop subscribing unless we mean to do what we say we will do. We are building our mansions in heaven everyday by what we do."[14] He was a "doer of the word," but coupled with his other-worldly perspective was an Arminian posture that human beings could in some way contribute to their own salvation.

Two years later, the NCMC gathered in Chicago. On Sunday, the convention's president introduced Elder H. L. Herod, who preached from Luke 19:13, "Occupy Till I Come," emphasizing "stewardship." "Courage and honesty are necessary to the proper use of our stewardship," he preached, adding,

> The ideals of God are in our trust, therefore Stewardship should be taken seriously. The ideals of Jesus, the Father of democracy and world peace, are the most precious possessions in our hand. Jesus died in defense of these ideals. The idea of accountability is contained in the Great Commission.[15]

During 1928, the Joint Executive Committee, after setting a goal to enroll 10,000 pupils in the national Bible school programs, urged each preacher to take advantage of the Church's pension plan to "protect himself and his family" during his declining years. The same committee recommended that letters be sent to the United Christian Missionary Society (UCMS) and to the board of directors or board of trustees of Butler University and the "rest of the schools

---

[13] Ibid., 21-22.
[14] *Minutes of the Tenth Annual Christian Missionary Convention of the Churches of Christ of the United States, August 23-29, 1926* (Louisville, Kentucky), 23.
[15] *Minutes of the Twelfth Annual Christian Missionary Convention of the Churches of Christ, August 25-September 2, 1928* (Chicago, Illinois): 7.

that practice discrimination."¹⁶ Preston Taylor and the NCMC were deeply concerned about elevating African Americans spiritually, while simultaneously knocking down racial barriers.

William Alphin, national field worker for the churches, reported that the spiritual and material conditions of congregations in Georgia, Missouri, South Carolina, North Carolina, and Texas all "showed improvement in organization and national cooperation." However, Texas, according to Alphin, was a "lead" state largely because of the presence and support of Jarvis Christian College. "I spent one month in Texas," Alphin testified, adding,

> At one time Texas was the leading state in reports to the General Work. Before and since Jarvis Christian College was placed in Texas this was true. Since the coming of Jarvis to Texas with its many needs and appeals, the efforts of many of the churches were turned to the needs of Jarvis. Report of the churches in Texas this year, as shown on the chart on the wall show Texas is coming again to its rightful place—IN THE LEAD.¹⁷

From August 26 to September 1, 1929, the Thirteenth Annual National Christian Missionary Convention met in Winston-Salem, North Carolina, a week before the official beginning of the Great Depression. The Women's Missionary Convention highlighted the conference, when delegates agreed to establish a memorial fund in the name of Jacob Kenoly, an African American missionary who tragically drowned while serving in Africa. The declaration read:

> In many of the sacrificed service rendered by our beloved Jacob Kenoly in Africa whose labors led the Christian Woman's Board of Missions into that field, be it remembered that we seek to perpetuate his spirit and passion to lift up Christ among the lowly by creating and maintaining a fund which will be known as the Kenoly Memorial Fund to be used to carry on some worthy missionary work, the nature of which may be worked out at the direction of the National Convention.¹⁸

---

¹⁶ Ibid., 10.
¹⁷ Ibid., 29–30.
¹⁸ *Minutes of the Thirteen Annual Christian Missionary Convention of the Churches of Christ, August 26–September 1, 1929* (Winston-Salem, North Carolina), 18.

Preston Taylor and African American Disciples of Christ eagerly and ardently cast their full support behind missionaries to Africa, but they did not advocate for the mass migration of black Americans to the motherland, as did controversial A.M.E. Bishop Henry M. Turner. Turner specifically yearned for the spiritual and economic uplift of the African continent. Historian Stephen Ward Angell explains Turner's position: "God, in his view, had ordained that black Americans suffer slavery in order to be civilized, made Christians, and return to Africa to convert their African brothers and sisters to Christianity." Turner, refuting the idolatry of whiteness and white supremacy, stirred more controversy in 1895, when he proclaimed that "God is a Negro."[19] Taylor was without question aware of Turner and his widespread influence, but he refused to endorse Turner's emigration posture or his declaration that God is black.

Notwithstanding their stark differences, the two men shared striking similarities. Both men were native Southerners. Turner was born free in South Carolina in 1834; Taylor was born enslaved in Louisiana in 1849. Both men served in the Union Army during the Civil War. Turner was a chaplain; Taylor, a drummer boy. Both men rose to prominent religious posts. Both were married four times, and both exerted tremendous influence on their respective denominations. Like Turner, Taylor solidified his place as a prominent leader among African American Disciples of Christ when he began writing for the *Christian Standard* in 1879 and when he organized the National Christian Missionary Convention in 1917. Taylor accomplished much good in and for his chosen faith tradition through the NCMC, but he did not do it alone. He relied on a biracial coalition of men and women to address topics to help make the Christian Church more effective generally.

When the 1930 National Christian Missionary Convention convened August 17–23, 1930, in Cleveland, Ohio, Taylor was in his declining years. Eight months later, he passed away at his home in Nashville, Tennessee, at the age of eighty-two. The "will of Preston Taylor" bequeathed all of his life insurance policies, cash, the family automobile, and personal property to his wife, Ida D. Taylor. "ITEM

---

[19] Stephen Ward Angell, *Bishop Henry McNeal Turner and African-American Religion in the South* (Knoxville, TN: University of Tennessee Press, 1992), 217, 228.

VI" in Taylor's will, notarized in 1925, reveals the heart of the black evangelist:

> I have been a Minister of the Christian Church for fifty-six years and am very much interested in the Christian education and training of young colored people, the missionary enterprises of my church, and the preaching of the Gospel at home and in foreign lands. I give and bequeath to the National Christian Missionary Convention, my library, containing many excellent books on theological subjects, and hope it may be placed in some school or college under the control of said religious corporation.
>
> My wife and my daughter are in comfortable circumstances and are not dependent upon my bounty, and both are in sympathy with my life work, and in the education and training of Christian teachers and missionaries.
>
> A corporation known as "National Christian Missionary Convention" is now being chartered and organized in Tennessee, (my wife and I being two of the nine incorporators), for the purpose of promoting religious education and benevolence at home and abroad, and for the purpose of cooperating with other like organizations of the Disciples of Christ in educating and maintaining teachers and missionaries, and in promoting the preaching of the Gospel.[20]

While Preston Taylor indulged in a plethora of extra-congregational activities—freemasonry, education, banking, and the funeral business—his first love was unquestionably preaching the word of God. He poured his energies and efforts into enterprise and left behind his material possessions to aid his chosen faith tradition in "educating and maintaining teachers and missionaries, and in promoting the preaching of the Gospel."

Ida Taylor carried out her husband's wishes until her death on March 10, 1947, in Nashville. Her funeral service was conducted at the Lea Avenue Christian Church before a large crowd. Four

---

[20] "The Will of Preston Taylor" (July 29, 1925), in DCHS Archives, Bethany, WV, 1-3.

years later, the city of Nashville honored Preston Taylor by naming an apartment complex after the religious and community leader. Designed to provide housing for low-income residents in Nashville, the dedicatory service was a fitting tribute to a man who devoted his life to feeding the hungry, attending to the incarcerated, and embracing the outcast. Preston Taylor, upon obtaining monetary and materials resources through grace and grit, used his bounty to bless and better the lives of others.

Preston Taylor served proudly as a drummer boy in the Union Army from 1864 to 1867. His experience as a Union soldier profoundly shaped his future endeavors (Disciples of Christ Historical Society, Bethany, West Virginia).

The above photo appears in William J. Simmons' book: *Men of Mark: Eminent, Progressive and Rising*. Simmons' description of Preston Taylor was accurate.

This historical marker in Nashville, Tennessee, commemorates the deaths of three African American firefighters—Charles C. Gowdy, Harvey Ewing, and Stokely Allen—who died in 1892 tragically while trying to put out a fire. Preston Taylor's leadership after this tragedy catapulted him to regional and national fame (Photo by author).

Booker T. Washington (1856-1915), the esteemed leader of Tuskegee Institute in Tuskegee, Alabama, bestowed lofty praise on Preston Taylor in his 1906 book, *The Negro in Business*. Washington and Taylor knew and admired each other.

Preston Taylor organized Greenwood Cemetery in 1888 to provide African Americans in Nashville proper and dignified burials (Photo by author).

David Lipscomb (1831-1917), longtime editor of the *Gospel Advocate* and contemporary of Preston Taylor, disagreed with Preston Taylor's decision to appoint new elders at the Gay Street Christian Church on the basis of "popular vote." This conflict prompted Taylor to organize the Lea Avenue Christian Church in Nashville, Tennessee, in 1891 (Disciples of Christ Historical Society, Bethany, West Virginia).

Workers in Greenwood Park preparing caskets for Preston Taylor's Funeral Company (Disciples of Christ Historical Society, Bethany, West Virginia).

Greenwood Cemetery with the Fountain Square in the center (Disciples of Christ Historical Society, Bethany, West Virginia).

Visitors at Greenwood Park patronizing "Grandma's Kitchen," where food was served. Black Nashvillians frequented the Park for festivals, fairs, and other leisure activities (Disciples of Christ Historical Society, Bethany, West Virginia).

Georgia Gordon Taylor (1856-1913), one of the original Fisk Jubilee Singers, was Preston Taylor's third wife. Their marriage lasted twenty-three years before her untimely death in 1913 (Disciples of Christ Historical Society, Bethany, West Virginia).

Gravesite for George Gordon Taylor at Greenwood Cemetery (Disciples of Christ Historical Society, Bethany, West Virginia).

Ida Mallory Taylor (1878-1947), married Preston Taylor in 1916. A gifted musician and Bible teacher, Mrs. Taylor stood by her husband's side until his death in 1931 (Center for Restoration Studies, Abilene Christian University, Abilene, Texas)

Gravesite for Preston Taylor (1849-1931) at Greenwood Cemetery which he established in 1888 (Photo by author).

Epilogue

'He Led the Way'

He becometh poor that dealeth with a slack hand: but the hand of the diligent maketh rich.
—Proverbs 10:4

Charge them that are rich in this world, that they be not highminded, nor trust in uncertain riches, but in the living God, who giveth us richly all things to enjoy; that they do good, that they be rich in good works, ready to distribute, willing to communicate; laying up in store for themselves a good foundation against the time to come, that they may lay hold on eternal life.
—1 Timothy 6:17-19

Preston Taylor, born and reared in a presidential family in the tumultuous pre-Civil War era, served as a drummer boy in the Union Army and emerged victorious with freedom and fire in his bones. Such unforgettable experiences fired his passion to pave the way for his people as a railroad contractor, an educator, and an evangelist. More than an ordinary preacher, he was a versatile man who channeled his skills and energies into various enterprises, including education, freemasonry, banking, the YMCA, and others.

While compiling biographical sketches of renowned African American leaders such as Richard Allen, Crispus Attucks, Benjamin Banneker, Frederick Douglass, Robert Smalls, and others in his book, *Men of Mark: Eminent, Progressive, and Rising*, William J. Simmons, a noteworthy black educator and author, said that Preston Taylor "is a man who will impress you when you meet him as thoroughly in earnest. He is never idle, always with new plans, warm hearted, generous, sympathetic and a true brother to all men who deserve the cognizance of earnest, faithful workers for Christ."[1]

Taylor remained an active civic leader and energetic churchman until his death on Monday, April 13, 1931, at 3:25 PM at his home at Greenwood Park. He was eighty-two years old. Significantly and symbolically, he died a month after the adoption of "The Star-Spangled Banner" as America's national anthem; he passed away two weeks after the fierce anti-lynching advocate, Ida B. Wells, died. And he died one week after the Scottsboro Boys went on trial in Alabama. All of these pivotal events attest that Taylor died at a time when scores of Americans celebrated the American flag, symbolizing the nation's birth of freedom, yet for many African Americans, freedom remained elusive. On one hand, most white Americans rejoiced over the adoption of "The Star-Spangled Banner" as the official national anthem; on the other hand, African Americans generally sorrowed over the passing of Ida B. Wells. Yet, except for residents of Middle Tennessee, Taylor died with little acclaim or fanfare.

Additionally, Preston Taylor passed away six months before celebrated inventor, Thomas Edison, died. Indeed, when Edison died, an emotional President Herbert Hoover announced: "He multiplied light and dissolved darkness."[2] What Edison did for the world physically, Taylor achieved for African Americans socially and spiritually. Taylor, of course, lacked the global renown that Edison garnered; still, many Middle Tennessee residents and members of the Christian Church (Disciples of Christ) lauded the evangelist because "he led the way"[3] for his people in Nashville and beyond.

He led the way as a drummer boy in the Union Army. He led the way as a railroad contractor in getting black laborers hired in the railroad industry. He led the way as an editor in guiding African American Disciples through the pages of the *Christian Standard.* He led the way in 1892, when the three black firefighters perished in a Nashville fire. He led the way by creating Greenwood Cemetery and thereby bestowing dignity on a people often spurned by the broader white community. In a segregated environment, he led the way in forming Greenwood Park, a recreational park and a

---

[1] William J. Simmons, *Men of Mark: Eminent, Progressive, and Rising* (New York: Arno Press, 1968), 300–301.

[2] Cited in Edmund Morris, *Edison* (New York: Random House, 2019), 11.

[3] Simmons, *Men of Mark*, 298.

"breathing place" for African Americans. The establishment of these two facilities, among other feats, marked the minister as a man of spiritual and social action. Other African American leaders—such as Frederick Douglass, Booker T. Washington, and Ida B. Wells—might have attained more renown through their impressive feats, public pronouncements, and prolific writings; and they might have been more erudite in learning and more eloquent in their speech. But few earned the reputation of being a "doer of the word."

Preston Taylor was first and foremost a committed Christian and an earnest adherent of the Christian Church. His involvement in Freemasonry afforded him opportunities to aid widows, orphans, and strangers; such extra-congregational organizations were merely expressions and extensions of his faith in Jesus. While he dabbled in youth organizations, economic enterprises, and educational efforts, his primary passion was local pastoral ministry, and the Lea Avenue Christian Church in Nashville was, without question, his pride and joy.

Taylor was a contemporary of Frederick Douglass and Booker T. Washington, both of whom (like Taylor) were products of biracial unions in the South. The death of Douglass in 1895 bequeathed the leadership crown to Washington for the next two decades, until his death in 1915. Yet the acclaimed Tuskegee educator honored Taylor when he included a biographical sketch of his impressive feats in his 1906 book, *The Negro in Business*. Another contemporary source called Taylor an "iron" man with a compassionate heart. The "Lord prospered him" to acquire material resources, which he subsequently used to feed the hungry, clothe the naked, care for orphans and widows, and bury the dead. His four marriages suggest that he struggled with marital fidelity. Still, he was "rich in good works." And despite his many transgressions, he toiled to pave the way for his people.

Bibliography

Newspapers

Christian Monitor (Washington, D.C.), 1882.
Christian Standard (Cincinnati, Ohio), 1879–1884, 1911.
Daily American (Nashville, Tennessee), 1892.
Gospel Advocate (Nashville, Tennessee), 1888, 1907.
Gospel Plea (Edwards, Mississippi), 1911.
Harper's New Monthly Magazine (1845).
Louisville Daily Courier (Louisville, Kentucky), 1867.
Nashville Banner (Nashville, Tennessee), 1931.
Nashville Globe (Nashville, Tennessee), 1906–1918.
The Tennessean (Nashville, Tennessee), 1912.

Articles and Books

Abrahams, James L. *The Men of Secession and the Civil War, 1859-1861*. Wilmington, DE: Scholarly Resources, 2000.

Ambrose, Stephen E. *Nothing Like It in the World: The Men Who Built the Transcontinental Railroad, 1843-1869*. New York: Simon & Schuster, 2000.

Anderson, James D. *The Education of Blacks in the South, 1865–1935*. Chapel Hill, NC: University of North Carolina Press, 1988.

Angell, Stephen Ward. *Bishop Henry McNeal Turner and African-American Religion in the South*. Knoxville, TN: University of Tennessee Press, 1992.

Arnesen, Eric. *Brotherhoods of Color: Black Railroad Workers and the Struggle for Equality*. Cambridge, MA: Harvard University Press, 2001.

Baker, Ray Stannard. *Following the Color Line: An Account of the Negro Citizenship in American Democracy*. New York: Doubleday, 1908.

Bauer, Jack. *Zachary Taylor: Soldier, Planter, Statesman of the Old Southwest*. Baton Rouge, LA: Louisiana State University Press, 1985.

Blight, Dwight W. *Frederick Douglass' Civil War: Keeping Faith in Jubilee.* Baton Rouge, LA: Louisiana State University Press, 1989.

Blight, Dwight W. *Race and Reunion: The Civil War in American Memory.* Cambridge, MA: Harvard University Press, 2001.

Bodenhorn, Howard. "The Mulatto Advantage: The Biological Consequences in Rural Antebellum Virginia." *Journal of Interdisciplinary History* 33 (Summer 2002): 21–46.

Boydston, Jeanne, et al. *Making a Nation: The United States and Its People.* combined ed. Upper Saddle River, NJ: Prentice Hall, 2002.

Brands, H. W. *T. R.: The Last Romantic.* New York: Basic Books, 1997.

Burnley, Lawrence A. Q. *The Cost of Unity: African-American Agency and Education in the Christian Church, 1865–1914.* Macon, GA: Mercer University Press, 2008.

Butler, Anthea D. *Women in the Church of God in Christ: Making a Sanctified World.* Chapel Hill, NC: University of North Carolina Press, 2007.

Canellos, Peter S. *The Great Dissenter: The Story of John Marshall Harlan, America's Judicial Hero.* New York: Simon & Schuster, 2021.

Cato, Willie. *His Hand and His Heart: The Wit and Wisdom of Marshall Keeble.* Winona, MS: J. C. Choate, 1990.

Cherok, Richard J. *Debating for God: Alexander Campbell's Challenge to Skepticism in Antebellum America.* Abilene, TX: Abilene Christian University Press, 2008.

Collier-Thomas, Bettye. *Jesus, Jobs, and Justices: African American Women and Religion.* New York: Alfred A. Knopf, 2010.

Commager, Henry Steele, ed. *The Civil War Archive: The History of the Civil War in Documents.* New York: Black Dog & Leventhal, 2000 [1950].

Dickens, Charles. *A Tale of Two Cities.* South Naples, FL: Trident Press International, 2000 [1859].

Du Bois, W. E. B. *The Souls of Black Folk.* New York: Signet Classics, 2012 [1903].

Egerton, John. *Nashville: The Faces of Two Centuries, 1780–1980.* Nashville, TN: PlusMedia, 1979.

Ellsworth, Scott. *Death in a Promised Land: The Tulsa Race Riot of 1921.* Baton Rouge, LA: Louisiana State University Press, 1982.

Farmer, James. *Lay Bare the Heart: An Autobiography of the Civil Rights Movement.* Fort Worth, TX: Texas Christian University Press, 1985.

Fee, John G. *Autobiography of John G. Fee, Berea, Kentucky.* Chicago: National Christian Association, 1891.

Foner, Eric. *Reconstruction: America's Unfinished Revolution.* New York: Harper & Row, 1988.

Foner, Philip S., ed. *Frederick Douglass: Selected Speeches and Writings.* Chicago: Lawrence Hill Books, 1999.

Foster, Douglas A., Newell D. Williams, Paul Blowers, and Anthony L. Dunnavant. *The Encyclopedia of the Stone-Campbell Movement.* Grand Rapids, MI: Eerdmans, 2004.

Fox, William K., ed. *The Untold Story: A Short History of Black Disciples.* St. Louis, MO: Christian Board of Publication, 1976.

Franklin, John Hope. *The Autobiography of John Hope Franklin.* New York: Farrar, Straus and Giroux, 2005.

Franklin, John Hope, and Evelyn Brooks Higginbotham. *From Slavery to Freedom: A History of African Americans.* New York: McGraw-Hill, 2011 [1947].

Garrett, Leroy. *The Stone-Campbell Movement: The Story of the American Restoration Movement.* Joplin, MO: College Press, 2006 [1981].

Gilkes, Cheryl Townsend. *"If It Wasn't for the Women": Black Women's Experience and Womanist Culture in Church and Community.* Maryknoll, NY: Orbis Books, 2001.

Goetsch, Elizabeth K. *Wicked Nashville.* Charleston, SC: The History Press, 2017.

Gorman, James L. *Among the Early Evangelicals: The Transatlantic Origins of the Stone-Campbell Movement.* Abilene, TX: Abilene Christian University Press, 2017.

Hamilton, Holman. *Zachary Taylor: Soldier of the Republic.* Indianapolis: Bobbs-Merrill, 1941.

Harlan, Louis R. *Booker T. Washington: The Wizard of Tuskegee, 1901–1915.* New York: Oxford University Press, 1983.

Harrell, David Edwin Jr. *Quest for a Christian America: The Disciples of Christ and American Society to 1866.* Nashville, TN: Disciples of Christ Historical Society, 1966.

Harrell, David Edwin Jr. *Sources of Division in the Disciples of Christ, 1865–1900: A Social History of the Disciples of Christ.* vol. 2. Tuscaloosa, AL: University of Alabama Press, 2003 [1973].

Harris, William C. *Lincoln and the Border States: Preserving the Union*. Lawrence, KS: University Press of Kansas, 2011.

Harvey, Paul. *Freedom's Coming: Religious Culture and the Shaping of the South from the Civil War Through the Civil Rights Era*. Chapel Hill, NC: University of North Carolina Press, 2005.

Higginbotham, Evelyn Brooks. *Righteous Discontent: The Women's Movement in the Black Baptist Church, 1880–1920*. Cambridge, MA: Harvard University Press, 1993.

Hiltzik, Michael. *Iron Empires: Robber Barons, Railroads, and the Making of Modern America*. Boston: Mariner Books, 2021.

Holloway, Karla F. C. *Passed On: African American Mourning Stories*. Durham, NC: Duke University Press, 2002.

Hopkins, C. Howard. *History of the YMCA in North America*. New York: Associated Press, 1951.

Hughes, Richard T. *Reviving the Ancient Faith: The Story of Churches of Christ*. Abilene, TX: Abilene Christian University Press, 2008 [1996].

Humble, Bill. *Campbell and Controversy: The Story of Alexander Campbell's Five Great Debates with Skepticism, Catholicism, and Presbyterianism*. Joplin, MO: College Press, 1986.

Hunter, Tera. *Bound in Wedlock: Slave and Free Marriage in the Nineteenth Century*. Cambridge, MA: Harvard University Press, 2017.

Isaac, Paul E. *Prohibition and Politics: Turbulent Decades in Tennessee, 1885–1920*. Knoxville, TN: University of Tennessee Press, 1965.

Jones, Jacqueline. *Labor of Love, Labor of Sorrow: Black Women, Work, and the Family, from Slavery to the Present*. New York: Vintage Books, 1986.

Kazin, Michael. *A Godly Hero: The Life of William Jennings Bryan*. New York: Alfred A. Knopf, 2006.

Kendi, Ibram X. *Stamped from the Beginning: The Definitive History of Racist Ideas in America*. New York: Hachette Book Group, 2017 [2016].

King, Martin Luther Jr. *Strength to Love*. Philadelphia: Fortress Press, 1981 [1963].

Lavender, David. *The Great Persuader*. Boulder, CO: University Press of Colorado, 1998 [1969].

Levine, Bruce. *Thaddeus Stevens: Civil War Revolutionary, Fighter for Racial Justice*. New York: Simon & Schuster, 2021.

Lincoln, C. Eric, and Lawrence H. Mamiya. *The Black Church in the African American Experience.* Durham, NC: Duke University Press, 1990.

Logan, Rayford W., and Irving S. Cohen. *The American Negro: Old World Background and New World Experience.* Boston: Houghton Mifflin, 1970 [1967].

Lovett, Bobby L. *A Black Man's Dream, The First One Hundred Years: The Story of R. H. Boyd.* Bobby L. Lovett, 1993.

Lovett, Bobby L. "From Winter to Winter: The Afro-American History of Nashville, Tennessee, 1870–1930." Unpublished manuscript, 1981.

Lovett, Bobby L. *The African-American History of Nashville, Tennessee, 1780–1930.* Fayetteville, AR: University of Arkansas Press, 1999.

Lucas, Marion B. *A History of Blacks in Kentucky, Volume 1: From Slavery to Segregation, 1790–1891.* Frankfort, KY: Kentucky Historical Society, 1992.

Lyda, Hap. "A History of Black Christian Churches (Disciples of Christ) in the United States Through 1899." PhD diss., Vanderbilt University, 1972.

Madigan, Tim. *The Burning: Massacre, Destruction, and the Tulsa Race Riot of 1921.* New York: Thomas Dunne Books, 2001.

Marrs, Elijah P. *Life and History of Rev. Elijah P. Marrs, First Pastor of Beargrass Baptist Church and Author.* CreateSpace. www.docsouth.unc/neh/marrs

McAllister, Lester G., and William E. Tucker. *Journey in Faith: A History of the Christian Church (Disciples of Christ).* St. Louis: Bethany Press, 1975.

McKinley, Silas Bent, and Silas Bent. *Old Rough and Ready: The Life and Times of Zachary Taylor.* New York: Vanguard Press, 1946. McMurry, Linda O. *To Keep the Waters Troubled: The Life of Ida B. Wells.* New York: Oxford University Press, 1998.

McPherson, James M. *Battle Cry of Freedom: The Civil War Era.* New York: Oxford University Press, 1988.

Meier, August, and Elliott Rudwick. "Negro Boycotts of Jim Crow Streetcars in Tennessee" *American Quarterly* 21 (Winter 1969): 755–763. Moore, William D. "Riding the Goat: Secrecy, Masculinity, and Fraternal Jinks in the United States, 1845–1930." *Winterthur Portfolio* 41 (Summer/Autumn 2007): 161–188. Morris, Edmund. *Edison.* New York: Random House, 2019.

Morton-Young, Tommie. *Nashville, Tennessee: Black America Series.* Charleston, SC: Arcadia Books, 2000.

Northup, Solomon. *Twelve Years a Slave.* New York: Dover Publications, 1970 [1854].

Ownby, Ted. *Subduing Satan: Religion, Recreation, and Manhood in the Rural South, 1865–1920.* Chapel Hill, NC: University of North Carolina Press, 1990.

Pinn, Anne H., and Anthony B. Pinn. *Fortress Introduction to Black Church History.* Minneapolis: Fortress Press, 2002.

Pinn, Anthony B. *Introducing African American Religion.* New York: Routledge, 2013.

Potter, David. M. *The Impending Crisis, 1848–1861.* New York: Harper & Row, 1976.

Rabinowitz, Howard N. *The First New South, 1865–1920.* Arlington Heights, IL: Harlan Davidson, 1992.

Redkey, Edwin S., ed. *Grand Army of Black Men: Letters from African-American Soldiers Union Army, 1861–1865.* New York: Cambridge University Press, 1992.

Richardson, Clement, ed. *The National Cyclopedia of the Colored Race.* Montgomery, AL: National Publishing Company, 1919.

Robbins, Faye Williams. "A World-Within-A-World: Black Nashville, 1880–1915." PhD diss., University of Arkansas, 1980.

Robinson, Edward J., ed. *A Godsend to His People: The Essential Writings and Speeches of Marshall Keeble.* Knoxville, TN: University of Tennessee Press, 2008.

Robinson, Edward J. *Show Us How You Do It: Marshall Keeble and the Rise of Black Churches of Christ in the United States, 1914–1968.* Tuscaloosa, AL: University of Alabama Press, 2008.

Robinson, Edward J. *To Lift Up My Race: The Essential Writings of Samuel Robert Cassius.* Knoxville, TN: University of Tennessee Press, 2008.

Robinson, Edward J. *To Save My Race from Abuse: The Life of Samuel Robert Cassius.* Tuscaloosa, AL: University of Alabama Press, 2007.

Sears, Richard D. *Camp Nelson, Kentucky: A Civil War History.* Lexington, KY: University Press of Kentucky, 2002.

Sears, Richard D. *The Day of Small Things: Abolitionism in the Midst of Slavery, Berea, Kentucky, 1854–1864.* Lanham, MD: University Press of America, 1986.

Shank, Harold. "Nashville's Central Church of Christ: The First Twenty Years." *Restoration Quarterly* 41 (1999): 11–26.
Sidbury, James. *Becoming African in America: Race and Nation in the Early Black Atlantic.* New York: Oxford University Press, 2007.
Simmons, Todd W. "Preston Taylor: Seeker of Dignity for Black Disciples." *Discipliana* 60 (Winter 2000): 99–109.
Simmons, William J. *Men of Mark: Eminent, Progressive, and Rising.* New York: Arno Press, 1968.
Smith, C. C. *The Life and Work of Jacob Kenoly.* Cincinnati, OH: Methodist Book Concern, 1912.
Smith, Suzanne E. *To Serve the Living: Funeral Directors and the American Way of Death.* Cambridge, MA: Belknap Press of Harvard University, 2010.
Stampp, Kenneth M. *The Peculiar Institution: Slavery in the Antebellum South.* New York: Vintage Books, 1956.
Waller, William, ed. *Nashville in the 1890s.* Nashville, TN: Vanderbilt University Press, 1970.
Ward, Andrew. *Dark Midnight When I Rise: The Story of the Jubilee Singers Who Introduced the World to the Music of Black America.* New York: Farrar, Straus and Giroux, 2000.
Washington, Booker T. *The Negro in Business.* New York: AMS Press, 1971 [1907].
Weeks, Terry, and Bob Womack. *Tennessee: The History of an American State.* Montgomery, AL: Clairmont Press, 1996.
Wheeler, Richard. *Witness to Appomattox.* New York: Harper & Row, 1989.
White, Deborah Gray. *Ar'nt I a Woman? Female Slaves in the Plantation South.* New York: W. W. Norton, 1985.
White, Jonathan W. *A House Built by Slaves: African American Visitors to the Lincoln White House.* New York: Rowman & Littlefield, 2022.
Wiley, Bell Irvin. *The Life of Billy Yank: The Common Soldier of the Union.* New York: Doubleday, 1971.
Williams, Charlotte A. *The Centennial Club of Nashville: A History from 1905–77.* Nashville, TN: Centennial Club, 1978.
Williamson, Joel. *New People: Miscegenation and Mulattoes in the United States.* New York: Free Press, 1980.
Wright, George C. *Life Behind a Veil: Blacks in Louisville, Kentucky, 1865–1930.* Baton Rouge, LA: Louisiana State University Press, 1985.

Zimring, Carl A. *Clean and White: A History of Environmental Racism in the United States.* New York: New York University Press, 2015.

Index

A

Allen, Richard, 157
Allen, Stokely H., 81, 152
Allison, J. H., 106
Alpha Kappa Alpha, 127
Alpha Phi Alpha, 127
Alphin, William, 139, 140, 143, 145, 146, 148
American Missionary Association (AMA), 15
Armstrong, Mrs., 90
Attucks, Crispus, 74, 157
Atwater, Anna, 130
Ayers, A. M., 46
Ayers, H. M., 34, 35, 51, 53

B

Babcock, Clara Hale, 46
Baker, Ray Stannard, 67
Banks, Mary, 55
Banneker, Benjamin, 157
Batterson, Fanny, 54
Battle, Fannie, 77
Bent, Silas, 4, 7
Berea College, 14, 29
Berry, H. S., Sr., 36, 37, 38, 39, 40, 95, 96, 111
Birth of a Nation, 63, 127
Blackburn, Deesy L., 145
Bliss, Betty (Taylor), 5
Bostick, Sarah Lue, 46
Boyd, Crawford, 28
Boyd, Henry A., 107
Boyd, R. H., 103, 107
Boydston, Jeanne, 141, 142
Brands, H. W., 73
Brayboy, H. Jackson, 25
Brindle, D. A., 119
Brooks, Fisher, 68
Brooks, Jesse, xi

Brooks-Summer Affair, 6
Brownsville Race Riot, 66, 73
Brown, W. H., 29, 37
Bryan, William J., 74
Buckner, Samuel, 33, 52
Buffalo Soldiers, 135
Burch, D. T., 115
Burnley, Lawrence A. Q., 132, 133
Butler University, 147

C

Campbell, Alexander (black preacher), 114
Campbell, Alexander (white preacher), xv, 35
Campbell, Mrs. Alexander (wife of black preacher), 56
Camp Nelson (Kentucky), 11, 12, 14, 15
Carr, Benjamin, 107
Carroll, Chief, xi, xii
Carter, Ellen, 56
Carter, Lizzie, 50
Caruthers, A. G., 82, 83
Cassius S. R., 11, 25, 114, 131, 132
Cave, Reuben Lindsay, 112, 113, 114, 115
Center for the Study of Negro Life, 128
Chesapeake and Ohio Railroad, 23
Christian Baptist, 35, 116
Christian Standard, 6, 17, 27, 28, 29, 30, 31, 33, 34, 35, 36, 37, 38, 39, 44, 45, 46, 48, 49, 50, 51, 52, 53, 54, 55, 56, 57, 95, 96, 119, 149, 158
Clansman, 63, 64, 65
Clarke, Henry, 50
Clay, Henry, 129
Cockrill, Aaron, xi
Coleman, Ann, 28, 55
Combs, J. C. M., 71
Combs, Micah S., 79, 80, 81, 82, 93
Compromise of 1850, 6
Conrad, Rufus, 113, 117
Cooper, Lillian, 116
Cowan, Thaddaeus, 111, 112
Craig, Mary, 55
Crawford, J. P., 101
Cross, Alexander, 135

D

Davis, Jefferson, 16, 17
Davis, R. H., 137
Dawson, Stephen, 27, 28

Dickerson 146
Dickerson, W. H., 117, 122, 133, 138, 146
Dixon, Jr., Thomas, 63, 65
Dixon, Phoebe, 55
Douglass, Charles, 10
Douglass, Frederick, 3, 8, 10, 11, 98, 157, 159
Douglass, Lewis, 10
Dred Scott Case, 6
Du Bois, W. E. B., xvi, 53, 68, 74, 103
Duke, Mercy, 120
Dunbar, Paul Laurence, 69, 70
Dye, R. J., 119

E

Edison, Thomas, 158
Elam, E. A., 77
Ellington, W. S., 75
Emancipation Proclamation, 10, 72, 90
Errett, Isaac, 27
Ewing, Hardy, xi, xii, 81
Ewing, Robert, 105

F

Farmer, James, 53
Fee, John G., 9, 11, 12, 13, 14, 29
Ferrell, Ethel M., 116
First Great Migration, 145
Fisher, James, 46
Fisk, Clinton B., 98
Fisk University, 68, 89, 98, 106, 108, 120
Foraker, Joseph B., 74
Ford, Henry, 141
Franklin, John Hope, 22, 24, 63, 68, 73, 80, 100, 128, 134, 138, 142
Frazier, Annie, 31
Freedmen's Bureau, 21

G

Gano, John Allen, 130
Garden, James A., 67
Garfield, James A., 29, 30
Giddens, R. M., 112, 114
Gilkes, Cheryl, 47
Goetsch, Elizabeth K., 78, 97
Gooch, Margaret, 83
Gordon, George, 88, 90, 104, 114, 115, 120, 121, 122, 155
Gospel Advocate, 77, 97, 99, 112, 113, 114, 153

Gould, Sabine, 127
Gowdy, Charles C., xi, xii, xiii, 81, 152
Grant, Ulysses S., 16, 17
Graves, J. C., 28, 33, 34, 35, 44, 51, 55, 95, 96
Graves, W. D., 65, 66
Green, Nettie, 83
Greenwood Cemetery, xiii, 79, 81, 82, 83, 92, 93, 153, 154, 155, 156, 158
Greenwood Park, xiii, 69, 79, 82, 84, 85, 86, 87, 88, 90, 91, 92, 93, 104, 115, 121, 122, 123, 154, 158
Grubbs, Rosa Brown, 142, 145
Guild, George, xii

H

Hale, William J., 107, 108
Hall, Prince, 100
Harlan, John Marshall, 6, 7
Harlan, Lizzie, 66
Harrell, David Edwin, 40
Harrison, William H., 4
Hart, Dock A., 68, 102
Hatcher, Eugene, 90
Haynes, G. E., 75
Haynes, William, 98
Hays, William Shakespeare, 15, 16
Henderson, Florence, 56
Herod, H. L., 128, 147
Higginbotham, Evelyn Brooks, 22, 24, 47, 63, 68, 73, 80, 100, 128, 134, 138, 142
Hoffman, Anna (Preston Taylor's second wife), 26, 44
Holloway, Karla F. C., 84
Hopson, Winthrop A., 25
Houston, John G., 112, 114
Howse, Hilary Ewing, 76
Hughes, Bedford, 112
Humphrey, Ora, 66
Hunter, Tera, 45
Huntington, Collis P., 23, 24

J

Jackson, Andrew, 4, 83, 106
Jarvis Christian Institute, 136, 143
Jarvis, Ida V., 136
Jefferies, Jim, 69
Jefferson, Thomas, 7, 90
Jocelyn, Simeon S., 14
John Brown's Raid, 6

Johnson, A. N., 74, 75
Johnson, Bettie, 28, 55
Johnson, Jack, 69, 70
Johnson, James Weldon, 138, 141
Johnson, J. Rosamond, 141
Johnston, John T., 130
Jones, Annie, 28
Jones, Jacqueline, 47
Jowett, William, 28

K

Kansas-Nebraska Act, 6
Keeble, Marshall, 99, 116, 131, 132
Keith, Hardy, 76
Kennedy, J. B., 83
Kenoly, Jacob, 119, 135, 136, 148
Kenoly Memorial Fund, 148
Kenoly, Ruth, 119
King, Benjamin, 31, 37, 55, 56
King, Caroline, 54
King, Susie, 48, 57
Kirby, D. H., 76
Ku Klux Klan, 63, 101, 127

L

Lane Theological Seminary, 12
Langston, Arthur D., 83
Lard, Moses, 133
Last Will and Testament of the Springfield Presbytery, 30
Lawrence, William, 112
Lee, C. H., 56
Lee, Robert E., 17
Lehman, J. B., 119, 142
Lemon, Laura Pearl, 124
Lincoln, Abraham, 10, 17, 68, 90
Lincoln, C. Eric, xvi
Lincoln-Douglas Debates, 6
Lipscomb, David, 77, 97, 98, 99, 112, 113, 114
Locke, Alaine, 141
Louisville and Chattanooga Railroad, 23
Louisville Bible School, 25, 37
Lovett, Bobby L., xiv, 62, 81, 82, 87, 97, 98, 111
Lowery, Peter, 39
Lowery, Samuel, 39
Lowrey, John B., 15
Lowrey, William L., 15

Lucas, Marion B., 12, 13, 21
Lum Grade School, 25
Lunenburg Letter, 14, 116
Lyda, Hap, 26, 113, 114

M

Maccalla, William, 31
Malone, William, 66
Mamiya, Lawrence H., xvi
Marrs, Elijah P., 13
Martin, W. P., 143
Mayfield, R. L., 74, 104
McCulloch, J. E., 77
McFadden, Clara, 56
McGovern, R., 66
McKinley, Silas Bent, 4, 7
McPherson, James M., 15, 16
Meier, August, 62
Mexican-American War, 4
Millennial Harbinger, 115, 116
Moore, George W. (Ella Shepherd), 120
Moss, P. H., 143, 145
Muckley, G. W., 137
Murphy, M. J., 66

N

Napier, James C., 83, 87, 103, 104, 107, 108, 118, 134, 137
Nashville American, xi, 64
Nashville Banner, 6, 64, 67, 128
Nashville Globe, xiii, 54, 61, 62, 63, 64, 65, 66, 67, 68, 69, 70, 71, 72, 73, 74, 75, 76, 82, 83, 85, 86, 87, 88, 89, 90, 91, 92, 99, 100, 101, 102, 103, 104, 105, 106, 107, 108, 109, 115, 116, 117, 118, 119, 120, 121, 122, 123
National Association for the Advancement of Colored People (NAACP), 68, 89, 103, 128
National Baptist Publishing Board, 69, 92
National Christian Missionary Convention (NCMC), xv, 124, 128, 134, 135, 136, 137, 138, 140, 144, 147, 148, 149
National Christian Woman's Board (NCWB), 130, 131, 148
National Negro Business League, 73, 103, 104
National Urban League, 128
Negro in Business, The, 26, 69, 104, 153, 159
New Castle Bible School, 24, 25, 41
Nichol, William, 112
North Star, The, 3, 8
Northup, Solomon, 4, 5

O

One Cent Savings Bank and Trust, 103
Ownby, Ted, 84, 97

P

Page, Sarah, 142
Patterson, Malcolm Rice, 86, 89
Pearl High School, 108
Pearson, R. E., 128, 129, 130, 137
Plessy v. Ferguson (1896), 79
Polk, James K., 83
Pool, Thomas, 111, 112
Power, F. D., 51
Price, J. C., 98
Price, Maggie, 55

R

Rabinowitz, Howard N. 80
Red Summer, The, 138
Richardson, William C., 15
Robinson, M. F., 29
Rogers, Samuel, 130
Roosevelt, Theodore, 66, 73, 135
Rowland, Dick, 142
Rudwick, Elliott, 62
Russell, James C., 65
Ruth, George Herman "Babe," 141
Ryman Auditorium, 105, 106

S

Sand Creek Address and Declaration (1889), 40
Sanders, Martha, 55
Schell, Clara, 50, 51, 52, 56
Schell, W. H., 51
Scott, W. A. 133
Shepherd, Ella (Mrs. George Moore), 120, 122
Sidbury, James, 100
Siege of Petersburg, 16
Simmons, William J., 23, 26, 152, 157, 158
Smalls, Robert, 157
Smith, Green Clay, 29
Smith, Harry G., 135, 143
Smith, Martha, 51
Smith, Suzanne E., 83, 84
Southern Christian Institute (SCI), 25, 29, 119

Spradling, Ella (Preston Taylor's first wife), 26, 123
Springfield Race Riot, 68, 127
Stearns, M. J., 138
Stone, Barton W., xiv, xv, 30, 130
Stowe, Harriet Beecher, 64
Sullivan, Thomas Valentine, 105

T

Taft, William H., 74
Taylor, Anna (Preston Taylor's second wife), 44, 45, 57
Taylor, Betty (Preston Taylor's mother), 5, 44
Taylor & Company Undertakers, 81
Taylor, Ella (Preston Taylor's first wife), 26, 44, 123
Taylor, Errett Mitchell (Preston Taylor's infant son), 45
Taylor, Georgia Gordon (Preston Taylor's third wife) 88, 90, 104, 114, 115, 120, 121, 122, 155
Taylor, Hattie Whitney (Preston Taylor's infant daughter), 45
Taylor, Ida Mallory (Preston Taylor's fourth wife), 104, 122, 123, 149, 150, 156
Taylor, Major, 69, 70
Taylor, Margaret, 5
Taylor, Preston,
    Admiration of Booker T. Washington, 68, 69, 103
    Attends National Christian Missionary Convention (NCMC) in Cincinnati, OH, 146
    Attends National Christian Missionary Convention (NCMC) in Chicago, IL, 145, 147
    Attends National Christian Missionary Convention (NCMC) in Hawkins, TX, 143
    Attends National Christian Missionary Convention (NCMC) in Indianapolis, IN, 144
    Attends National Christian Missionary Convention (NCMC) in Louisville, KY, 147
    Attends National Christian Missionary Convention (NCMC) in Winston-Salem, NC, 148
    Background as enslaved person, 1-7
    Birth, 1
    Civil War experience, 9-17
    Commendation by Booker T. Washington, 69, 104
    Conflict at Gay Street Christian Church, 111-115
    Death, 6, 158
    Edits "Our Colored Brethren" column in *Christian Standard,* 27-32
    Establishes Lea Avenue Christian Church, 113
    First wife (Ella Spradling), 44
    Foreign missions, 119
    Fourth wife (Ida Mallory), 104, 122-124

Funeral service for fire-fighters, xii-xiii, 81
Greenwood Cemetery, 82-84
Greenwood Park, 84-93
Helps poor in Nashville, 75-78
Hosts National Christian Missionary Convention (NCMC) in Nashville, 128-140
Influenced by John G. Fee, 11, 13-15
Masonic work, 99-102
New Castle Bible School, 24-30, 41
Parents, 5-6
Pastoral ministry in KY, 26-30
Politics, 73-75, 95-99
Prohibition movement, 95-99
Race relations in Nashville, TN, 61-78
Railroad worker, 23-24
Relation to Zachary Taylor, 5-7
Role of women in the Christian Church, 43-57
Second wife (Anna Hoffman), 44-45
Tennessee Agricultural and Industrial State Normal School for Negroes (Tennessee State University), 107-109
Third wife (Georgia Gordon), 120-122
Tour of the Deep South, 70-73
Union Transportation Company (UTC), 62
Young Men's Christian Association (YMCA), 104-107
Taylor, Preston G. (infant son), 120
Taylor, Zachary, 4, 5, 6, 7
Taylor, Zed (Preston Taylor's father), 5, 6
Tennessean, xi, 76, 77, 119
Tennessee Agricultural and Industrial State Normal School for Negroes (Tennessee State University), 108
Tennessee Central College, 98
Tennessee Colored Fair Association (TCFA), 87, 88, 89, 90
Thomas, George, xi
Thomas, James, 34, 136
Todd, Martha, 28
Tohee Industrial School (Oklahoma), 25
Toombs, Robert, 74
Turner, Henry McNeil, 124, 149
Tyree, Evans, 91, 115, 118

U

Uncle Tom's Cabin, 6, 64
United Christian Missionary Society, 147
United States Colored Infantry (116th USCT), 11, 15, 16, 17, 22
United Transportation Company, 62, 78

W

Wadkins, Daniel, 39, 40
Walker, Madam C. J., 70, 149
Ward, Stephen Angell, 124, 149
Warfield, Clary, 28
Washington, Booker T., 23, 26, 67, 68, 69, 70, 73, 103, 104, 128, 135, 146, 153, 159
Washington, George, 4, 100
Waters, Jane, 46
Watkins, Miss, 90
Watkins, R. E., 71
Watkins, Solomon, 112
Watts, Isaac, 141
Wayman, Harriet, 124
Wells, Ida B., 80, 158, 159
Whaley, Margaret, 28
Wharton, A. D., 112, 114
White, Deborah Gray, 47
White, George L., 120
Wickliffe, Louisa, 55
Wilkins, D. R., 32, 33, 35, 38, 39
Wilkins, W. C., 104
Williams, J. B., 111, 112
Williams, Nancy, 54
Wilmot, David, 3
Wilmot Proviso, 3
Wilson, Woodrow, 63, 139
Womack, M. F., 36
Womack, S. W., 36, 38, 99, 116
Woman's Christian Temperance Union (WCTU), 97
Wood, Ann, 5
Woodson, Carter G., 128
Work, J. W., 76
World War I, 102, 106, 108, 128, 134, 137, 138, 139, 140
Wright, George C., 21, 22

Y

Young Men's Christian Association (YMCA), 104, 105, 106, 108, 109, 157

www.ingramcontent.com/pod-product-compliance
Lightning Source LLC
Chambersburg PA
CBHW050110170426
43198CB00014B/2516